I0083694

# Revolutionary Overthrow of Constitutional Orders in Africa

## Carlson Anyangwe

*Langaa Research & Publishing CIG*
*Mankon, Bamenda*

*Publisher*

*Langaa* RPCIG

Langaa Research & Publishing Common Initiative Group
P.O. Box 902 Mankon
Bamenda
North West Region
Cameroon
Langaagrp@gmail.com
www.langaa-rpcig.net


Distributed in and outside N. America by African Books Collective
orders@africanbookscollective.com
www.africanbookcollective.com



*ISBN: 9956-727-78-4*


© Carlson Anyangwe 2012

# Table of Contents

**Chapter 1: Introduction**..............................................1
Coup in the then Republic of Transkei..............................2
Meaning of coup d'état....................................................7
Armed rebellion as old as history....................................8
Monarchy, early target of coups.......................................9
Farcical incompetence in some coup attempts.....................10
Coup, shortcut to political power....................................11

**Chapter 2: The Military, a Frankenstein Monster**.............15
The military, regime security and national security.................15
Contested subordination of the military to civilian control.........19
Strategies for asserting control over the military....................23
Joint civil-military rulership............................................26

**Chapter 3: Why Overthrow a Government**.....................29
Practical considerations...............................................29
Theoretical bases......................................................33
Coup typologies......................................................37

**Chapter 4: How to Stage a Coup**...............................43
Prior agreement on important immediate matters...................44
Strategic control of the capital; emergency measures..............44
Judges and civil servants.............................................46
Coup by the executive...............................................48

**Chapter 5: Coups and the International Community**..........53
Attitude of international organizations generally.....................53
Attitude of Western countries generally.............................55
Attitude of the African Union specifically...........................56

**Chapter 6: Grundnorm and Revolutionary Legality**............ **63**

Grundnorm and the hierarchy of norms.............................63

Grundnorm and coup d'état...........................................66

Hierarchy of norms and revolutionary destruction of the
Grundnorm.............................................................69

Further explication of the meaning of grundnorm...................70

Possibility of legal void following a coup...........................73

Authority and legitimacy of usurper government...................74

International law and recognition of the usurper government......75

National constitution and military coup...........................76

**Chapter 7: Usurper Government: Its Legitimacy and the
Validity of its Acts**..................................................... **81**

Judges and the overthrow of government............................81

Legitimacy of the usurper government.............................88

De jure status of usurper regime: the doctrine of effectiveness.....89

De facto status of usurper regime: the doctrine salus populi suprema
lex.....................................................................92

**Chapter 8: Facing the Coup Challenge in Africa**............... **95**

What to do about coups..............................................95

What to do with Africa's military.....................................98

What to do with Africa's despotic executives.......................105

Coup counter-measures..............................................106

Case for coups.......................................................108

Case against coups...................................................110

**Chapter 9: Countries Where the Military Have Not Seized
Power (Yet)**............................................................. **115**

Where no attempt has ever been made.............................115

Where a coup or insurgency attempt has failed....................116

**Chapter 10: Countries Where the Military Have Seized Power
Once (So Far)**........................................................**129**

**Chapter 11: Countries Where the Military Have Seized Power More than Once**..........................................................135

**Chapter 12: Epilogue: Neo-patrimonial Governance and Revolutionary Overthrow of Governments in Africa**.......... 177
The rise of the neo-patrimonial state in Africa...................... 178
Continuing democracy and good governance deficit................ 181
Soldiers gun for political power.................................... 185

**Bibliography**............................................................ 187

# Pictures

Political map of Africa.................................................. ix

Coup and non-coup countries........................................... 13

Soldiers on patrol following a coup..................................... 23

Bemused civilians watch soldiers following a coup................. 28

Soldiers manning a street corner following a coup................. 42

Military vehicle blocks street following a coup..................... 43

Ahidjo, Selassie, Bokassa, Sobhoza II.................................51

AU, UN, EU flags........................................................61

Hans Kelsen............................................................ 64

Hierarchy of norms pyramid............................................66

Inverted collapsible pyramid..........................................70

Soldiers chasing demonstrating civilians............................ 80

Scale, judges.......................................................... 87

Military mistreatment of civilians.................................... 105

AU Leaders............................................................ 106

Corporal chastisement of a civilian by a soldier..................... 112

Civilian being manhandled by soldiers.............................. 113

POLITICAL MAP OF AFRICA

# Chapter 1

## Introduction

Political governance in Africa has oscillated between a measure of disciplined multiparty politics at independence to one-party authoritarian rule in the 1970s/1980s; and then, between chaotic political pluralism and life presidencies since the 1990s. Africa's experience with constitutionalism has therefore not been a happy one in the half century since the onset of the Independence era in the late 1950s. In the early 1960s and 1990s successive waves of great enthusiasm greeted new constitutions providing for multi-party democracy, rule of law and human rights guarantees. But in most of Africa, immediately after each wave of enthusiasm, hopes were quickly dashed by systemic corruption; despotic, abusive rule; and pervasive military coups. Military coups are now widespread, frequent and repeated. At least 44 out of 53 African states have experienced at least one coup or one attempted coup. And there is no sign that coup business will decline anytime soon. As of 2004, West African states alone experienced 44 successful military coups, 43 often-bloody failed coups, at least 82 coup plots, 7 civil wars, and many other forms of political conflict.[1] The statistics for Africa as a whole are much higher and depressing, reflecting a continent in the throes of continuing deep crises of governance and security. No African student of law, constitutions, politics, governance and security can be indifferent to this dismal state of affairs.

The title of this book is *Revolutionary Overthrow of Constitutional Orders in Africa*, the same title of my Professorial Inaugural Lecture delivered at Walter Sisulu University, South Africa, in August 2010. The subject is at the intersection of three disciplines: jurisprudence

---

[1] PJ McGowan, 'Coups and Conflicts in West Africa, 1955-2004: Part I, Theoretical Perspectives', *Society & Armed Forces*, vol. 32, 2005, p. 5, 'Part II, Empirical Findings', *Society & Armed Forces*, vol. 32, 2006, p. 234.

and legal philosophy, constitutional law and power politics, and civil-military relations, that is, military security policy which is one aspect of national security policy.[2]

The subject is of interest in at least four ways. It problematizes the inescapable question of governance in the African continent. It challenges the democratization agenda in Africa - how does one democratize not only political governance but also the instruments of violence in the state? It also challenges African constitutional lawyers and policy makers to seek a constitutional model that addresses the enduring menace of the power of the gun in African affairs and the changing role of the military in African politics. Finally, it underscores concerns about sovereignty and national security.

My set purpose in this book is to contribute to a fuller understanding of the coup syndrome in African. To this end, I vigorously interrogate the place of coups in the governance of Africa, and I inquire into the relevance of Kelsen's theory of revolutionary legality in the context of coup d'états in Africa.

## Coup in the then Republic of Transkei

One of the first legal challenges of a military coups in Africa was in respect of the coup d'état in the then Bantustan in South Africa known as Republic of Transkei. In Mthatha, which used to be the capital of that defunct Republic, there was in December 1987 a revolutionary overthrow of the Transkei government by coup d'état. That coup was followed by a bloody counter coup that failed. Wikipedia has the following entry:

> In 1987, there was a coup d'état led by General Bantu Holomisa, the then-leader of the *Transkei Defence Force*, the homeland's officially sanctioned military units. ... In 1990, Holomisa himself evaded a failed attempt to be ousted from his

---

[2] SP Huntington, *The Soldier and the State: The Theory and Politics of Civil-Military Relations*, Belknap Press, Harvard University, Cambridge Massachusetts, 1957; C Ferguson, *Coup d'état: A Practical Manual*, Arms & Armour Press, Dorset, 1987.

post, and when asked about the fate of his opponents, he claimed that they had died in the ensuing battles with *TDF* soldiers. It was later found that those deemed responsible for the foiled coup had only suffered minor injuries, but were subsequently executed without trial.

The *Times* of 5 April 1987 carried this report:

About 30 white mercenaries serving as military commanders and advisers in the black South African tribal homeland of Transkei have been arrested in an apparent mutiny by junior officers amid rumours of an attempted *coup d'état* there. Umtata, the capital of the nominally independent homeland, was reported by residents on Saturday to be tense, with hundreds of heavily armed soldiers and police patrolling the streets, manning roadblocks, guarding key installations and raiding the homes of government opponents. ... Mystery enveloped most of the developments, and government officials were unwilling to explain what was happening. Gen. Zondwa Mtirira, Defence Force commander, said simply, "I am out of the picture" when he was contacted by telephone in Umtata. Family members at the home of Brig. Bantu Holomisa, the chief of staff, who was freed from two months' political detention last week, said he was "at a soccer match" and not available.

About a month later the same newspaper on 12 May 1987 carried a report, in effect a footnote to the coup story of the previous month. The report appeared under the shouting headline *'South African Homeland Leader Banishes Brother to Village amid Coup Rumours'*:

With most of the 3,000-man army and many of the tribal chiefs appearing to back Kaiser Matanzima, Transkei government officials were talking Monday of a possible coup. The Johannesburg newspaper *Beeld* reported "rising fears that a civil war will break out shortly." The army's complaint against George

Matanzima, according to informed sources in Umtata, is that he spends most of his time womanizing and that government administration in the past year has all but collapsed in Transkei. ... A group of Transkei army officers last month freed a colleague, Brigadier Bantu Holomisa, the armed forces chief of staff, who had been detained on security charges. They then arrested and expelled 27 white mercenaries, most of them veterans of the old Rhodesian army, who had been their advisers. Holomisa replaced the army commander, who was forced into retirement, and at 31 he is now a major general.

But the facts that are relevant for the purpose of the subject at hand are authoritatively set out in the Transkei case of *Matanzima & Anor v The President of the Republic of Transkei & Anor*, judgment in which was delivered on 3 October 1988, almost a year after the coup. The case itself is reported in 1989 (4) SA 989 (TK). In their decision, Davies and Lombard, JJ detailed what happened, including the following account:

> The Transkei Constitution ... came into effect on the day of independence, 26 October 1976... At about noon on 30 December 1987, the second respondent [Bantu Holomisa], as Commander of the Transkei Defence Force, announced over the National Radio that martial law had been declared and the Constitution suspended. Soldiers under his command moved into the centre of Umata (the capital), helicopters flew over the city and army vehicles moved through the streets declaring the imposition of 'Military Rule'. Second respondent also announced that the country would be run 'in the interim' by an 'interim Government' consisting of a Military Council supported by an appointed Council of Ministers... On 31 December martial law was lifted, there being no civil unrest and no apparent threat of such unrest. On 5 January 1988, Decree 1 was published under a notice in the Government Gazette stating that the President had assented to it. The Decree, inter alia, dissolved the already

suspended Parliament, established a Military Council and a Council of Ministers to govern the country until restoration of civilian rule, empowered the President to make laws by decree for the peace, order and good government of Transkei, declared the courts incompetent to inquire into or to pronounce upon the validity of any decree, and directed that all courts and commissions lawfully established in terms of the existing laws shall continue to exercise jurisdiction and have the powers that they exercised and had hitherto."

The nub of the legal issue in *Matanzima* was whether or not the Transkei Military Government that came to power by coup d'état was legitimate and its decrees legally valid. The Court held that that Government even as an interim one was a revolutionary government for at least two reasons. First, it was firmly established and in no danger of being ousted. Second, its administration was effective and acquiesced in by the people. The Court therefore came to the conclusion that the Transkei Military Government was the lawful Government of the Republic of Transkei and its legislation legitimated *ab initio*.

The process by which the learned Justices arrived at this conclusion was this. The starting point was the important question whether the Transkei Military Government was legitimate; for if it was then its proclamations were legal. In order to answer this question the learned Justices first had to dispose of the preliminary question whether that Government was a revolutionary government. If it was not, then the 1976 Transkei Constitution survived the purported coup and, in terms of that constitutional order, the 'military government' would clearly be illegal and its laws invalid. But if the military regime was a revolutionary government then that meant the 1976 Constitution ceased to exist and the new government was not amenable to it but only to such laws as it would have itself seen fit to proclaim. Being the product of a revolution the Military Government would be legitimate. However, the legitimacy of that Government depended on two factors, (i) whether it was firmly established in the sense that it was in no danger of being ousted, and (ii) whether it was effective in the sense that it was accepted by the people.

The learned Justices opined that the government was firmly established and in no danger of being ousted. But it is submitted that the court erred in its appreciation of the reality of the prevailing situation. The government of any of the Homelands was at risk of ceasing to exist at any time. A binding resolution adopted by the UN General Assembly in 1977 declared 'independence' of any of the Homelands invalid and forbade recognition of any of them.[3] The Homelands therefore had only nominal independence. Further, the anti-apartheid forces within South Africa were successfully fighting for the re-integration of the Homelands into one united South Africa. Further still, the Transkei Military Government was always at risk of being sacked at any time by Pretoria. In Bophuthatswana, when Rocky Malabane-Metsing overthrew the government of Mangope in a military coup on 10 February 1988, Pretoria intervened and re-instated Mangope. PW Botha, President of apartheid South Africa at the time justified the intervention by declaring that the Government of South Africa was opposed in principle to the obtaining of power by violence.[4] Given this reality, any government in the Homelands clearly had only a temporary lease of life. The prospects of the ouster at any time, at least from without the Transkei, of the Military Government were therefore very real.

The learned Justices further reasoned that the Military Government was accepted by the people and therefore was effective. It would seem this conclusion was arrived at from the fact that the people of the capital did not come out to demonstrate against or oppose the military takeover. But a country is not just the capital city. Further, it is unrealistic to expect people to come out with bare hands

---

[3] UNGA Res A/RES/32/105N of 14 December 1977, adopted at the 102nd plenary meeting.
[4] 'South Africa Quells Coup Attempt in a Homeland,' *New York Times*, 11 February 1988. For an account of further unrest in the Homeland two years later, see 'Turmoil Spreads to 2nd Homeland,' *New York Times*, 8 March 1990.

to face an armed insurrectionary government determined to keep the power it has captured. In such circumstances, the people can do little more than acquiesce in the factual situation. But acquiescence or mere submission is one thing, consent or positive acceptance is another thing. Regrettably for Jurisprudence, these points were not canvassed by learned counsel for Applicants.

The points elicited in connection with *Matanzima* reflect some of the issues canvassed in this book. Those who lived through that eventful period of a coup, attempted coup and rumours of a threatened coup in the Transkei must have been divided on the necessity and expediency of the military overthrowing the civilian government and seizing power. Some must have been in favour and others against the coup. That is not surprising. Throughout the world and from ancient times to this day, a revolutionary overthrow of an established government always elicits similar reactions from the public.

## Meaning of coup d'état

The expression *'coup d'état'* is derived from French. It literally means a blow to the state. It is a blow to the state by the state's own military force. Analytically, the blow is not to the state as such but to the existing government. State is not the same thing as government. A government is simply an agency through which the state acts. That being the case the term 'coup d'état' would seem a misnomer. But the term has acquired the settle meaning of a sudden, often violent, and unconstitutional overthrow of an existing government by a small group. The small group infiltrates all or part of the armed forces and the police. It takes control and then uses the leverage thus gained to overthrow the government. A coup is thus described by some authors as "the infiltration of a small but critical segment of the state apparatus, which is then used to displace the government from its control of the remainder."[5] A coup merely results in the replacement

---

[5] E Luttwak, *Coup d'état: A Practical Handbook*, Harvard University Press, 1980.

of leading government officers and thus is a change in power from the top. It rarely alters a country's fundamental social and economic policies, and its foreign policy. It rarely results in a significant redistribution of power among competing sections of the country. In this respect a military coup may be contrasted with a typical revolution. A classic revolution is *usually* achieved by a large number of people working for basic social, economic, political and foreign policy change.[6]

The military establishment is an important tool for purposes such as asserting state authority, enforcing the rule of law, and protecting the state against external aggression. This is so because the military monopolises the state's instrument of physical force, being endowed as it is with an unrivalled capacity to project force. Ironically, it is this very power which, when not properly and carefully managed, can also pose a serious threat to civil authority as evidenced by the endless number of coups in Africa since the 1950s.

**Armed rebellion as old as history**

A revolutionary overthrow of the constitutional order of a state takes place when the constitution of that state is replaced by another one in a manner not prescribed by the constitution valid until then. In other words, an abrupt and drastic change of the prevailing legal order is effected by unconstitutional means. Examples of such means are a mass revolt of the people as seen in 2011 in Egypt, Libya and Tunisia; an executive coup d'état by the ruler himself; an armed insurgency; or, commonly, the application of force against the existing government by the country's own soldiers. Revolutionary accession to power is constitutionally impermissible universally. It is a rebellion and therefore ordinarily appears as a mere pathology. Yet the phenomenon is as old as history.

Throughout recorded history political governance has never been the reserved domain of the civil authorities. Because they have access

---

[6] Encyclopedia Britannica.

to and control the weapons of terror, soldiers and armed insurgents have periodically shot their way through to political power. History, ancient and modern, furnishes ample proof of this: Julius Caesar (Roman Empire), Oliver Cromwell (Britain), Napoleon Bonaparte (France), Mazzini and Garibaldi (Italy), Mao Tse-Dong (China), Kamel Ataturk (Turkey), Fidel Castro (Cuba), Francisco Franco (Spain), Charles de Gaulle (France), Spinola (Portugal), George Washington and the American Rebels (United States), Lenin and the Bolsheviks (Russia), the Sandinistas (Nicaragua), George Papadopoulos (Greece), and countless military coup-makers in Africa, Asia and Latin America. The only continents that have so far not experienced a coup d'état (yet) are North America (USA, Canada) and Australia.

## Monarchy, early target of coups

Out of the current 55 African States only nine have not experienced a successful or failed military coup or an armed insurgency. The nine states are Botswana, Djibouti, Malawi, Mauritius, Mozambique, Namibia, Swaziland, South Africa (post-apartheid), and Zimbabwe.

Early military coups in Africa were against monarchical rule. In 1952 Col. Neguib and Nasser overthrew King Farouk of Egypt. In December 1963 Zanzibar gained independence as a monarchy under an Arab Sultanate. Barely a month later, in January 1964, the Sultanate and his Government was overthrown in a bloody insurrection characterized as 'the Revolution'. In Rwanda the monarchy was overthrown and abolished in 1965. In Burundi Captain Micombero overthrew King Ntare V in 1966 and abolished the monarchy. In Uganda, in 1966 Prime Minister Obote ousted King Mutesa of Buganda. In 1969 Col. Muammar Gaddafi overthrew King Idris I of Libya. In 1974 the Armed Forces Committee (the Dergue) headed by Gen Aman Andom and Col. Haile Mariam Mengistu overthrew Emperor Haile Selassie of Ethiopia.

In each of these cases the coup-makers abolished the monarchy and proclaimed a republic. In this, in the overthrow of monarchies, the revolutionaries were merely following on the footsteps of others before them: the American rebels (1776-178) overthrew the British Monarchy in the American Colonies, the French Revolutionaries (1789) overthrew the French Monarchy, the Russian Revolutionaries (1917) overthrew the Czar, Primo de Rivera in 1931 overthrew Spanish King Alfonse XIII followed shortly afterwards by Francisco Franco's 1936-1939 destructive insurgency in that country, the Iranian Revolutionaries (1979) overthrew the Shah, and the Greek rebels led by Col. George Papadopoulos (1967) overthrew King Constantine.

There are three surviving monarchies on the African continent, the Kingdoms of Lesotho, Morocco, and Swaziland. Of these, only Swaziland has so far escaped a coup or an abortive coup. But how for how long these monarchies will survive is an open question.

## Farcical incompetence in some coup attempts

While successful forcible overthrow of governments has been quite common in Africa, there have also been cases of coups attempted with farcical incompetence, ending up in egregious failures. Examples of such abortive coups include the attempt against Julius Nyerere[7] (Tanganyika) in 1961; Leon Mbah (Gabon) in 1964; Haile Selassie (Ethiopia) in 1960; Joseph Desiré Mobutu (Zaire) in 1967, 1977, 1978; King Hassan II (Morocco) in 1971, 1972; Murtala Muhammad (Nigeria) in 1976; Agostinho Neto (Angola) in 1977; Daniel arap Moi (Kenya) in 1982; Kenneth Kaunda (Zambia) in

---

[7] Some commentators say it was a mere mutiny to get rid of the British officers in the Tanganyika army and not an attempted coup. But even so the mutiny was conducted in a very disorganized and incoherent manner. If anything, it was an example of military indiscipline and threat of political overthrow had the demands of the mutineers for promotion and better service conditions not been acceded to by government. See, Nestor Luanda, 'The Tanganyika Rifles and the Mutiny of January 1961', in Hutchful & Bathily (ed.), *The Military and Militarism in Africa*, CODESRIA, Dakar, 1998, p. 175.

1991; Paul Biya (Cameroun) in 1984; Frederick Chiluba (Zambia) in 1998; and several other incompetent and failed coups in Chad and Central African Republic in the last few years.

In some cases a failed coup does not discourage other soldiers from subsequently trying their luck. Usually the second or third attempt succeeds as in Ethiopia, Nigeria and Zaire. Generally, when a first attempt fails (Angola, Cameroun, Gabon, Kenya, Tanzania) and a second attempt also fails (Morocco and Zambia), the military is thereby shown as incompetent and cowardly. This has the effect of definitively discouraging any subsequent coup attempt.

## Coup, shortcut to political power

Is the coup syndrome symptomatic of something wrong with leadership and governance in Africa or with the African military establishment? Or is this a necessary phase in a trial-and-error search for an authentic African model of governance that ought to include the men and women whose profession it is to kill using weapons paid for by the taxpayer?

A coup is a meta-legal phenomenon. The consequences of the unconstitutional removal of an established government are severe. Failed coup perpetrators are always charged with treason. Successful coup perpetrators may find sanctions slammed against their military government by the international community or the African Union. This notwithstanding, potential coup makers have not been deterred and coups continue with frightening frequency. In every country of the world a bid to take over power by force of arms is a treasonable crime punishable capitally or with a long term of imprisonment. For the coup leaders, a failed bid could mean paying with their lives for their temerity. But so strong is the lure of political office that determined soldiers and insurgents are not put off by the risk of possible failure and the possibility of judicial or extra-judicial execution.

11

The failure rate of coups is low and the chances of success are at worst fifty-fifty.[8] It would thus appear that the 'game' is certainly worth the candle. The very fact of success is in itself a guarantee of impunity.[9] Besides, success means being propelled from the Spartan conditions of the barracks or from the harsh conditions of the bush to the lavish and lofty comfort of State House, the pinnacle of power in the state and which gives easy access to state coffers. Moreover accession to State House gives power to control other human beings. The usurper may even reap a bonus by being lionized and hero-worshipped as the 'saviour' or 'messiah'.

A military government monopolizes both political and gun power. This monopoly removes the possibility of any serious physical challenge to military rule. The military government abolishes the constitution valid until then. It promulgates a new and self-made constitution. It thereby guarantees its own impunity for carrying out the overthrow of the previous government. By taking these measures the usurper government also puts beyond the reach of judicial inquiry its legality or legitimacy and the validity of its acts.

Usurpers are very much alive to the illegality of their conduct. That is why they adopt measures to shield themselves and their regime from legal attack in the court of law. Such measures often succeed in shielding the usurpers' regime from direct legal challenge on the ground of unconstitutionality. But the measures have not always succeeded in preventing the legitimacy question cropping up incidentally. After a coup, the court, in the continuation of the normal discharge of its judicial functions, may be confronted with a case the resolution of which perforce requires it to pronounce itself

---

[8] P McGowan, 'African military coups d'état, 1956-2001: frequency, trends and distribution,' *Journal of Modern African Studies*, 41(3), 2003, p. 351; see also, N Ngoma, 'Civil-Military Relations: Searching for a Conceptual Framework with an African Bias,' in G. Chileshe et al (ed.), *Civil-Military Relations in Zambia*, Institute for Security Studies, Pretoria, 2004, p. 3.

[9] There is authority in at least one Commonwealth jurisdiction to the effect that once constitutional order is restored after a coup, the former usurpers of power can be tried and punished for high treason. See the Pakistani case of *Asma Jilani v. The Government of Punjab & Anor*, PLD 1972 SC 139.

on the legitimacy of the usurpers' regime and the validity of its laws. This legitimacy question has always been a dilemma for the courts. They have tended to deal with this thorny question by praying in aid a number of doctrines which then enable them to extricate themselves from what is clearly a knotty situation. More often than not, the new military regime gives short shrift to court rulings that declare the new government illegal or illegitimate.

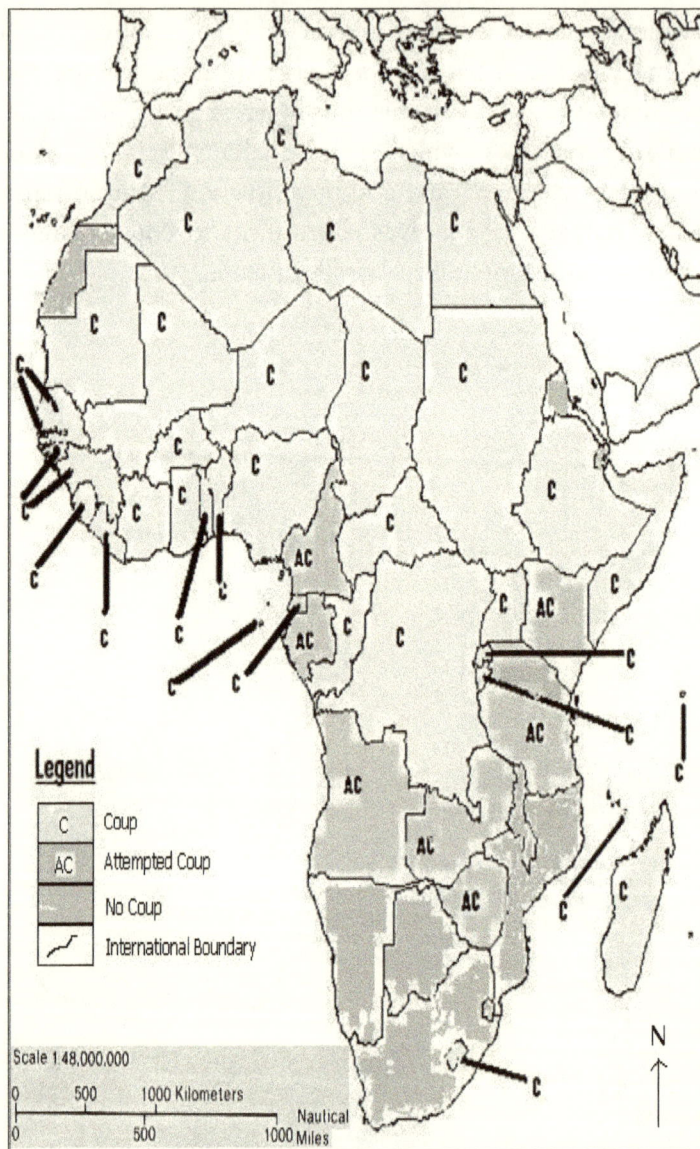

COUP and NON-COUP AFRICAN COUNTRIES

# Chapter 2

## The Military, a Frankenstein Monster

The generalized nature and frequency of coups in Africa puts into question the loyalty of the African military to the civil government. The frequency of coups also suggests that the African military is a deeply divided force since a coup is never the result of a unanimous decision by the armed forces. A house divided is a weak house. Thus 'military-led authoritarianism' and the 'militarization of the political function' in Africa probably suggest a creeping decay of the state in Africa and probably portend the eventual disintegration of the military institution itself.

### The military, regime security and national security

The frequency of coups also suggests that civil-military relations are poor and that there is deep distrust between the two.[10] As a result, no African government could possibly be sure that its orders would always be carried out by the military even though constitutionally the ruler is also the 'commander-in-chief' of the military forces. This situation puts the ruler in a dilemma because it implies that he is no more than a paper 'commander in chief'. In fact, any measure deemed by the military, or even just a section of it, to be ill-considered could act as the spark triggering a coup. In coup-prone countries, governments therefore tend to live in fear of the military and the ruler sleeps with one eye open.

---

[10] SP Huntington, *The Soldier and the State: The Theory and Politics of Civil-Military Relations*, Belknap Press, 1981; G Chileshe et al. (ed.), *Civil-Military Relations in Zambia*, Institute for Social Security, Pretoria, 2004; TS Cox, *Civil-Military Relations in Sierra Leone: A Case Study of African Soldiers in Politics*, Harvard University Press, Cambridge Mass., 1976.

In not a few African countries the distrust between soldiers and civilians remains a major concern. The attitude of soldiers towards the general population and vice versa is one of constant antagonism and despise. In many instances the military behave as an army of occupation and as though it can possibly live outside the wider society in a cloistered world of their own and by themselves. This inauspicious atmosphere is a pointer to extremely poor and unhealthy relations between the civilian population and the armed forces. In such circumstances it is very easy for any foreign army or even an insurgency to defeat the country's military as demonstrated by the ease with which Tanzanian forces literally marched into Uganda and defeated Amin's hated soldiers. It is a sad fact that in many African countries the military are not popular with local people and is seen and experienced as a force of oppression and extortion. This sort of atmosphere poses problems of both regime security and national security.

A coup removes a regime from power. But a coup could also trigger an internal insurgency or a civil war as happened in Nigeria, Burundi, Sierra Leone, and Liberia engendering refugee flows and internal displacement of persons. Moreover, a coup could have the unintended effect of 'inviting' external intervention. France has intervened in Gabon, Congo-Kinshasa, Congo-Brazzaville, Chad, Central African Republic etc. to re-instated unwanted incumbents. It has intervened in Central African Republic, Comoros and Côte d'Ivoire to remove incumbents it is unhappy with. Tanzania intervened in Seychelles to save the incumbent government from an unfolding coup and in Uganda to remove an unwanted military government. Senegal intervened in Gambia to save the incumbent government from a creeping coup. Nigeria intervened in Sierra Leone to re-instate a government ousted by a military coup.

In fact, a coup or insurgency could provoke hostility between neighbouring states as that between Sudan and Uganda provoked by the elusive Ugandan rebel group known as the Lord's Resistance Army. It could provoke cross-border raids as between Rwanda and Democratic Republic of Congo or even an inter-state conflict as in the case of the Uganda-Tanzania war in 1979[11] or the intervention of Ethiopia in Somalia in 2008.

This state of affairs further poses a human security problem in view of the fact that some governments use the military for ordinary policing as well. Despotic regimes further use the military as a tool to deprive citizens of their freedom and the enjoyment of other fundamental human rights. The result is that repression and brutality of the people follows. These actions incur and deepen still further the hatred and despise of the despot and his regime. That is not all. These actions also create a negative public perception and loathing of the military. The hostile, anti-government atmosphere thus created by military involvement in ordinary policing credibly explains why an insurgency is always so easy and successful. In many instances popular support for an insurgency arises because of the generalized experience of the government and the military as oppressors. The public then welcomes or even joins insurgents as 'liberators.'

In some countries the situation of insecurity is compounded by the constant mistreatment by soldiers of their own fellow citizens provoking civilian contempt for the military. Insecurity is also compounded by periodic insurgency uprisings as in Chad, Central African Republic, Uganda, Liberia, Democratic Republic of Congo, and, until recently in Burundi. Under such conditions the state becomes exposed to the dangers of external and internal threats. It was so easy for Tanzanian soldiers to move into Uganda and dislodge Idi Amin. It was so easy for Ethiopian soldiers to move into Somalia and dislodge the regime there. It was so easy for Nigeria to move into the British Southern Cameroons territory of the Bakassi Peninsula and dislodge the occupying troops of the French-speaking State of *République du Cameroun*. It was so easy for Libyan soldiers to move in and occupy the Chadian territory of the Aouzou strip. It was so easy for Laurent Kabila to defeat Mobutu's corrupt and ill-disciplined army, Mobutu himself escaping into exile where he eventually died. It

---

[11] SA Ochoche, 'The Military and National Security in Africa', in E Hutchful & A Bathily (ed.), *The Military and Militarism in Africa*, CODESRIA, 1998, p. 105.

was so easy for the Ivoirian insurgency to take over the northern half of Ivory Coast, occasioning for years a *de facto* partition of the country.

The American Revolutionaries were very perceptive. They showed repugnance towards quartering of soldiers among civilians. They were against military involvement in civilian law enforcement, arguing that soldiers are never to be used against their civilian countrymen.[12] They enunciated the principle that the military is not to be independent of and superior to the civil power. The Posse Comitatus Act, 1878, prohibited federal military personnel from engaging in domestic law enforcement activities, except in cases involving for example states of emergency, domestic unrest, and natural disasters. The later Posse Comitatus Act of 1970 also prohibits the use of soldiers for performing civil law enforcement missions. The Act provides:

> "Whoever, except in cases and under the circumstances expressly authorized by the Constitution or Act of Congress, wilfully uses any part of the Army or the Air Force as a *posse comitatus* or otherwise to execute the laws shall be fined not more than $10 000 or imprisoned not more than two years, or both."[13]

In Africa, by contrast, the situation is different. At independence African states inherited or created a standing army. The army was merely one of the trappings or outward symbols of statehood, like the coat of arms, the anthem, or the flag, to be used for ceremonial purposes. Over the years, however, African governments contrived to use the army to entrench themselves in power, to destroy political opponents, and to deprive citizens of freedom and other basic human rights. In many states the army has become a state

---

[12] Engdahl, 'Soldiers, Riots and Revolutions: The Use of Military Troops in Civil Disorders,' 57 *Iowa L. Rev.* 1, 28 (1971).

[13] 18 U.S.C. $1385 (1970); C I Meeks, 'Illegal law enforcement: aiding civil authorities in violation of the Posse Comitatus Act,' *Military Law Review*, vol. 70, 1975, p.83.

constabulary and the police have been militarized not only in training but also in weaponry, uniform and ranks. The distinction, if at all, between police officer and soldier has become increasingly very blurred. Not surprisingly, many coups are often a military-police joint venture.

From the moment the military tasted political power and realized it is sweet after all, they started lurking in the shadows of power ready to pounce at any moment.[14] This is a continuing threat hanging like the Sword of Damocles over the head of every African ruler. And so the military, initially created for ceremonial use and for external defence only, has become something of a Frankenstein monster, feared by government and citizens alike. In the circumstances, most African rulers have adopted two basic strategies to cling on to power. They tribalise the military, making it a virtual preserve or keeping it under the firm control of soldiers from their ethnic background. Further they co-opt military officers into the rulership. They resort to these expedients in the belief that their personal safety and the security of their regime would thereby be guaranteed. This has not always worked. The reason why it has not always worked is because of the abiding "love-hate, trust-mistrust relationship between the military and society on the one hand, and between the military and government on the other hand." [15]

## Contested subordination of the military to civilian control

In the idiom of military and political science the concept of civilian control of the military entails placing ultimate responsibility for a country's strategic decision-making in the hands of the civilian political leadership, rather than to professional military officers.[16]

[14] C Anyangwe, 'Good Governance, Democracy and Corruption in Africa', in R Simigiannis & C Letlojane (ed.), *Human Rights Theories and Practices*, HURISA, Johannesburg, 2001, p. 215.
[15] N Ngoma, 'Civil-Military Relations: Searching for a Conceptual Framework with an African Bias,' in G. Chileshe et al (ed.), *Civil-Military Relations in Zambia*, Institute for Security Studies, Pretoria, 2004, p. 3.
[16] http://en.wikipedia.org/wiki/Civilian_control_of_the_military.

Such civilian control of the military is considered a prerequisite feature of a stable society. "Our principle," Mao Zedong once said referring to the supremacy of the Chinese Communist Party in decision making in the state, "is that the Party commands the gun, and the gun must never be allowed to command the Party." In military matters as well it is civilians who make broad policy and strategic decisions and set broad goals. The responsibility of translating these into operational plans is then left to military commanders. For example, it is the civil authorities that determine the budgetary allocation for the military and exercise, through parliament, oversight of all defence and security matters. It is also the civil authorities and not the military that decide on the use of physical force because such use impacts on the national budget and other resources, on the citizens of the country and on inter-state intercourse. The civil authorities formulate policies, the military implement them. The purpose of the military, it has been said, is to defend society, not to define it.

When it comes to military technical matters, however, politicians rely on the advice of professional military commanders trained in the art and science of warfare to inform the limits of policy. The process of giving advice becomes a Trojan horse enabling the military establishment to enter the bureaucratic arena. Once inside that arena it starts advocating for or against a particular course of action such as increased military spending, repression of civilians, some robust action, etc. It starts shaping the policy-making process to its taste and blurring any clear-cut lines of civilian control.[17] The armed forces accept objective control by the civilian government in the sense that they do not necessarily challenge the position of the civilian government as the constitutionally supreme authority. But otherwise, they very much regulate and control their own affairs and, under the guise of professionalism, they retain the ability to act independently. Thus, when there is war or a state of war, military commanders

---

[17] Wikipedia.

dictate strategy and tactics, and the civilian leadership simply defers to what is believed to be their informed judgments.

It is clear though that if the military were to have full autonomy, to become independent of the civil power, they would easily use force or the threat of it to achieve their preferred goals. In many African countries institutional control over the army is weak or even absent. Moreover, soldiers claim military affairs as their own particular sphere of expertise and influence. They tend to consider this sphere to be a no-go area for civil authorities, a reserved domain.

African countries do not hesitate to use the military to crush domestic political opposition through intimidation or sheer physical force, and through interfering with the ability to have free and fair elections. And yet the proper role of the military domestically is to protect civilians in their complete enjoyment of fundamental human rights. The role of the military is not to destroy or otherwise maim or hurt civilians. Any military that accepts to be used to shoot at and kill civilians or otherwise hurt or terrorise them must be a criminal and cowardly military. One observer has noted that the unprincipled use of the military poses the paradox that "because we fear others we create an institution of violence to protect us, but then we fear the very institution we created for protection".[18]

The frequent coups in Africa and their attendant general hardships for the population bear out the caution given long ago by Elbridge Gerry. Gerry was delegate to the American Constitutional Convention. He cautioned that standing armies in time of peace "are inconsistent with the principles of republican Governments, dangerous to the liberties of a free people, and generally converted into destructive engines for establishing despotism." [19]

On their part, civilian leaders cannot challenge their militaries by means of force. Their control over the military may therefore be asserted only through a number of 'soft' methods. One such method is the familiar legal construct by which the head of state is

---

[18] PD Feaver. 1996. "The Civil-Military Problematique: Huntington, Janowitz and the Question of Civilian Control," 1996 *Armed Forces and Society* 23(2): 149-178.
[19] http://en.wikipedia.org/wiki/civilian

constitutionally made the commander-in-chief of the armed forces within the chain of command. In reality he is not the operational chief. Being commander-in-chief only means that ultimate political and policy decisions in the use of physical force lie with him.

Another traditional method of asserting civil control over the military consists in the age-old practice of establishing a distinct civilian police force and/or a militia with access to a limited range of weapons. Such a force, at least as originally designed, exists to mitigate, to an extent, the disproportionate strength that a country's military possesses. In some countries, for example in the US, civilians are allowed to possess and bear arms. The reasoning behind this arrangement, as in the case of a 'people's militia' or a *posse comitatus*, is that every qualified citizen is responsible for the defence of the nation and the defence of liberty, and that every such citizen would go to war, if necessary. In the US also, nuclear weapons, the ultimate instrument of terror and mass destruction, are owned by the civilian Department of Energy and, interestingly, not by the Department of Defence as one would have expected.

SOLDIERS ON PATROL FOLLOWING A COUP

## Strategies for asserting control over the military

Western countries emphasise an apolitical military under the control of a civilian government. Constitutionally, the armed forces come under the ultimate control of the state president and for that reason he is also given the title of 'commander-in-chief'. The military is also subject to parliamentary oversight. Thus, through its constitution, a legitimate democratic government demands obligatory obedience from the military. In a democracy, the armed forces accept such control because they are part of the system, which they have recognised. Totalitarian regimes on the other hand are apt to enforce civilian control through a variety of means such as patronage, terror, the deployment of political commissars as a form of subjective control[20], and even divisive strategies.

There is no unanimity of views on the question whether it is desirable to distinguish and keep the military as a body separate from the larger society. Proponents of an autonomous professional military officer corps[21] argue that it is the best way of asserting objective civilian control over the military. In their view, military autonomy conduces to political neutrality of the military. They also argue that such an arrangement inculcates in the military an *esprit de corps* and a sense of distinct military 'corporateness' that prevents political interference by soldiers.

But, there are those opposed to the creation and projection of the military as an autonomous 'species' of people trained to kill for a livelihood and living divorced from the rest of society. Opponents of the military as an autonomous species of citizens argue that the tradition of the citizen-soldier 'civilianizes' the military. For them 'civilianization' of the military is the best means of preserving the loyalty of the armed forces towards civilian authorities. In not a few African countries therefore the ranks in the police and correctional services are militarised. For example, one finds captains and generals not only in the military but also in these services. The effect of this is to blur the line between "civilian" and "military" leadership and so to deny the military monopoly over the use of those officer ranks.

A more invasive method used by some African regimes to assert control over the military involves general oversight of the military. Active monitoring of the military officer corps and of the military in general is carried out in two ways. Civilian intelligence officers may be detailed to keep tabs on the officer corps and other soldiers thought likely to cause trouble. Similarly, civilian advisers may be posted in the department of defence to 'advise' the military and keep an eye on the military establishment. Again, in some countries the

---

[20] H Lupogo, 'Civil-Military Relations and Political Stability in Tanzania,' (2001) 10 (1) *African Security Review* 33.
[21] SP Huntington, *The soldier and the state: The theory and politics of civil-military relations*, op. cit.

operational use of the military in a district or region requires the approval of both the local area official and that of the minister responsible for the armed forces, both of who are, as a rule, civilians.

Furthermore, the regular rotation of soldiers through a variety of different postings is another effective tool for reducing military autonomy. This strategy limits the potential for soldiers' attachment to any one particular military unit or commander. Again, some governments place responsibility for approving promotions of military officers with the civilian authority. There, promotions are done by presidential decree or proclamation, a power he uses for patronage purposes and for making appointments based on ethnicity or tribal balance and not necessarily on merit.

The typical strategies used by most African countries for civilian control over the military are those that have been used by and perfected in Kenya and Cameroon Republic since independence. These methods include ethnic manipulation, politicization, and bribery. They also include giving to the military privileges of all kinds especially to the officer corps, and the establishment of a powerful paramilitary police as a counterweight to the military. The methods furthermore include the fragmentation of the military into various somewhat antagonistic 'special' units with nebulous and duplicating functions. In such an environment each unit believes or is made to believe it is more important than the other. Each one competes for the President's attention. Each one claims entitlement to the lion's share of the budgetary allocation for national security.

But these strategies have done little, notes one commentator, to institutionalize and entrench civilian control. They have moreover not entailed military professionalization, military autonomy, political insulation, and regime legitimization policies. In the view of the commentator these strategies are to be avoided if democratic civilian control of the military is to take root on the continent.[22]

---

[22] B N'Diaye, 'How not to Institutionalize Civilian Control: Kenya's Coup Prevention Strategies, 1964-1997,' *Society & Armed Forces*, vol. 28, 2002, p. 619.

Civilian control of the military forms the normative standard in societies other than military dictatorships. However, the practice of that control has often been the subject of pointed criticism from both military and non-military observers. Critics object to what they view as the undue 'politicization' of military affairs through elected officials. They also object to political appointees micro-managing the military. For critics, what is required of civilian officials is that they give goals and objectives to the military generals and leave the military to decide how best to carry out those orders. Critics argue that by placing responsibility for military decision-making in the hands of civilians (persons not professional in military affairs) the dictates of military strategy become subsumed to the political. This, critics conclude, has the effect of unduly restricting the fighting capabilities of the nation's armed forces for what should be immaterial or otherwise lower priority concerns.[23]

## Joint civil-military rulership

Military and insurgency take-over of government in Africa have become the rule rather than the exception. It is the shortcut to political power. All but a handful of African States have experienced an insurgency take-over, a military coup, or an attempted military coup. The message is clear. African soldiers have refused to accept their subordination to the civil authorities. They have refused to accept fully the hallowed principle of civilian supremacy in politics. Even in countries where soldiers have not yet usurped political power they have contrived to control the political life of the country indirectly. They are physically very visible throughout the country and

---

[23] CM Desch, *Civilian Control of the Military: The Changing Security Environment,* Johns Hopkins University Press, 2001; PD Feaver, *Armed Servants: Agency, Oversight, and Civil-Military Relations,* Harvard University Press, 2005; SE Finer, *The Man on Horseback: The Role of the Military in Politics.* Transaction Publishers, 2002; M Janowitz, *The Professional Soldier,* Free Press, 1964.

at state or regional functions. In fact, they are ubiquitous. They exercise a great deal of influence in the governance of the country.

Every African ruler is very alive to the ubiquity of the military and their monopoly of the gun. He therefore sleeps with one eye open and knows he must pander to the whims and caprices of the soldiers, lest something happens. The ruler is alive to the fact that not even his aide-de-camp or personal assistant or even his bodyguards can be fully trusted. Not a few African leaders have been killed by their own bodyguards. But there is hardly very much he can do in the circumstances. Many face this tricky situation by appealing to ethnic solidarity for protection. They hire as aides-de-camp and bodyguards soldiers or police officers from their ethnic region or extended families, or those initiated into the same esoteric society as the ruler himself. For example, it is believed that Freemasons, Rosicrucians, and members of various other mystical associations and occult fraternities pledge to protect and defend each other. But these expedients are never fool proof.

In order to minimize the risk of overthrow there has now emerged a trend towards joint civilian-cum-military governance of the country. Increasingly civilian heads of state are co-opting soldiers into the government, the diplomatic service, state agencies or corporations, and into policy-making institutions. Military chiefs are very conspicuous at all state functions both at national and local levels. In fact, some commentators observe that many African militaries have assumed a range of political roles since independence[24] and that as a result budgetary, institutional, training, and doctrinal devices will be needed to prevent military coups and political infringement.[25]

---

[24] SE Finer, *The Man on Horseback: The Role of the Military in Politics*, Transaction Publishers, 2002.
[25] E Hutchful, 'Demilitarising the Political Process in Africa: Some Basic Issues,' *African Security Review*, 1997. (http://www.iss.co.za/pubs/ASR/6No2/Hutchful.html

Likewise, a military head of state does not rule alone. He does not only depend on the ruling military council or committee that is usually set up following a coup. He also depends on the valued assistance of certain civilian constituencies. He depends on the middle class educated elite serving in the public and in the diplomatic services. He depends on the civilians, including those denoted as intellectuals, co-opted into the cabinet. A military regime would probably not last a single day in power in the absence of this critical collaboration. Left to themselves, the *lumpenmilitariat* would probably not survive a single day.[26]

BEMUSED CIVILIANS WATCH SOLDIERS FOLLOWING A COUP

---

[26] "The *lumpenmalitariat*," writes Ali Mazrui, "is that class of semi-organized sub-Westernized rugged and semi-literate soldiery which had begun to claim a share of power and influence in certain African states." See, A Mazrui & M Tidy, *Nationalism and New States in Africa*, East African Educational Publishers, Nairobi, 1984, p.261.

# Chapter 3

## Why Overthrow a Government

The strategic objective of gaining political power through the barrel of the gun (whether by the armed forces of the state or an armed insurgency fighting the established government) is to assume and use political power. In this sense, all coups, whether premeditated or not, are politically inspired. However much coup-makers may seek to hide their motives under a veil of altruistic discourse, reasons of self-interest are always present.

### Practical considerations

Rebels who take over government by force of arms always advance altruistic reasons for their treasonable action. The invocation of selfless reasons for taking over power is an attempt by the rebels to pass for reformers (if not 'liberators' or 'messiahs', at least 'development dictators') with a self-appointed mandate to effect sweeping economic, social and political reforms. But behind the altruistic reasons pleaded in justification of the take-over, however, self-interests always loom large.

#### 1.1 Altruistic rhetoric

The selfless reasons often given for the overthrow of a government include the claim that the ousted regime is guilty of one or more of the following crimes: tribalism, nepotism, mismanagement, economic plunder, corruption, misrule, ineptitude, inability to deal with the country's problems, abuse of power, interference with the judiciary, mal/non-development, establishment of a *de facto* or a *de jure* life Presidency.

The charge that an incumbent has established a life presidency by eliminating term limits means in effect that the incumbent President has overstayed his welcome and that regime fatigue has set in.[27] Overstay in power and authoritarian rule were the reasons given for the overthrow of Nkrumah (who was hardly in office for ten years), Mobutu, Macias Nguema, Bokassa, Moussa Traore, and Sékou Touré's successor. In this context, change by coup would appear as something of a welcome extra-constitutional practice or a convention dictated by necessity for effecting regime change in Africa in the face of life presidencies and despotic rule.

Corruption is the commonly pleaded reason for the overthrow of African regimes. A regime makes itself a good candidate for a coup d'état when it creates in the country an environment where bribery and graft become endemic and systemic. A regime also makes itself a good candidate for a coup when the State President and members of his regime become guilty of a consistent pattern of looting of the national treasury, the stolen money being stashed abroad as is often the case. Such a situation is in fact one of an officially-organized banditry, a situation in which the state has become bandit.

Misrule is a blanket word that covers practices such as tribalism, ethnic or sectional domination, autocracy, and massive human rights abuse. This is the reason most often advanced for overthrowing a regime. Just as the ethnic or tribal factor has always been crucial in the configuration of the military in African States, that same factor is always a critical element in almost any coup or insurgency take-over.

Lack of development, poverty and government ineptitude are surprisingly seldom advanced these days as justification for a coup or for taking to the bush. But these reasons did prompt Nasser's coup in Egypt, Gaddafi's coup in Libya, Mengistu's coup in Ethiopia, Rawling's coup in Ghana, Doh's coup in Liberia, and Gen. Verissimo Conneia Seabra's coup in Guinea-Bissau in 2003. Further, the lavishly

---

[27] Examples are: Moi's Kenya, Biya's Cameroun, Libya's Gaddafi, Mubarak's Egypt, Tunisia's Ben Ali, Obiang Nguema's Equatorial Guinea, Bongo's Gabon where incumbents contrived to prolong their tenuous and controversial stay in power for over a quarter of a century. Between January and April 2011 Ben Ali of Tunisia, Mubarak of Egypt and Gaddafi of Libya were overthrown by popular national revolts. An attempt in February 2011 to overthrow Biya of Cameroun through a similar revolt was violently crushed by the military.

paid and equipped Praetorian Guard in most African countries and the common use of the military for ordinary policing conduce to military coups.

Many African countries do not have clear and effective constitutional methods of changing government. Worse, attempts to change government through constitutional means have proved impossible. The fundamental constitutional problem and the challenge is that of working out a way of effecting regime change in a continent where many incumbents are determined to cling to power for life by unconstitutional means. Some incumbents have refused to accept the concept of limited government and have manipulated the 'constitution' so as to prolong their stay in power for an indefinite period.

*1.2 Reasons of self-interest*

Although coup makers never say so, it is clear that some coups are prompted by reasons of self-interest. There have been cases where the military have taken over power because they desire to improve the common lot of soldiers. Such coups are always staged by the lower or middle ranks of the army. For example, the Doh, Rawlings, and Sankara coups were in part prompted by the desire to give the military a better deal. In 2009, a section of the South African Defence Force staged a violent strike calling for improved conditions for soldiers. Had South Africa not been a democratic society underpinned by a robust Constitution creatively enforced by a strong and fearless judiciary it is conceivable that the disaffected soldiers would have staged a coup rather than go on strike.

Some coups are staged to counter or pre-empt some unwelcome measure, actually taken or only contemplated, by the State President against the military or any of its chiefs. For example, when President Nyerere tried to introduce the concept of a people's militia in Tanzania so as to break the military's monopoly of the state's instrument of terror and as an antidote to the phenomenon of military coups, Tanzanian soldiers mutinied and Nyerere owed his survival to foreign intervention. When Modibo Keita also tried to

31

create a people's militia in Mali, Moussa Traore overthrew him and seized power.

In The Gambia, the attempted coup against Sir Diawara in the 1980s was aimed at forestalling a perceived measure against the army. The attempt was crushed thanks to the intervention of Senegalese and British troops but Diawara was finally overthrown in the late 1990s by Captain Yahya Jameh. In Uganda, Idi Amin pre-empted Obote's planned action against him by staging a coup that ousted Obote from power. In Ghana, Rawling's co-conspirators pre-empted Government action against Rawlings by staging a coup and releasing him from jail to head the new military government.

In Guinea-Bissau, when the President presumed to sack General Asumana Mané on charges of aiding and abetting the Casamance insurgency in Senegal, the General rallied troops loyal to him and after months of fighting troops loyal to the President succeeded in overthrowing the Government in 1999. General Asumana was himself subsequently overthrown by Verissimo Seabra in 2005, blown to pieces by a bomb. In Guinea Conakry the military usurper, Moussa Dadis Camara, inaugurated his rule by mass killings in a football stadium. The killings attracted international opprobrium and sanctions against the leadership of the military regime. Shortly afterwards, the usurper ruler was himself shot in the head by his own *aide de camp* (ADC).

In some cases an ethnic armed insurgent group or an ethnic faction of the military has staged a coup against the established government so as to preserve or break the hegemony of the ethnic group that was in power. Rwanda (General Kagame), Burundi (Col. Buyoya), Cameroun (Captain Saleh), Uganda (Yoweri Museveni) and Nigeria (Major-General Gowon) provide edifying examples.

Whenever it has occurred, an insurgency take-over (which is always preceded by a long period of civil war) is in most cases the result of a struggle for power between opposing forces, one seeking to hold on to power and the other seeking to capture it by force. After a period of waging a bush war the rebel forces in Uganda (Yoweri Museveni), Congo Brazzaville (Sassou Nguesso), Democratic

Republic of the Congo (Laurent Kabila), Chad (Goukouni Ouéddei, Hissene Habre, Idriss Derby), Liberia (Charles Taylor), and Rwanda (Paul Kagame) eventually overthrew the established government in each of those countries and took over power.

Algeria, Angola, Burundi, Cameroun, Central African Republic, Ethiopia and Sierra Leone have also seen insurgency struggles. Other insurgency struggles have been cases of self-determination claims: Southern Sudan, Cassamance, the Western Sahara, and Eritrea. Of these, Eritrea and Southern Sudan have won their independence. In October 2011 the UN through its Committee for Decolonization reiterated the right of the people of the Western Sahara to self-determination.

**Theoretical bases**

Forcible overthrow of government is illegal in terms of the constitution valid before its overthrow. So what are the possible foundations for such action?

*2.1 Religion*

From a religious perspective, a faith-based government could arguably be dislodged if it loses its moral and religious compass and veers towards beliefs, customs and practices that are religiously indefensible. Based on the authority of the teachings of Paul in the book of Romans, Christians reason that the mission of government is to serve Christ no matter whether a government is conscious or unconscious of this mission. That is why the Bible urges Christians to yield to rulers.[28] It therefore stands to reason that if a government ceases to serve Christ, if it ceases to be guided by Christian faith, values and principles it may be subverted and a new one amenable to serving Christ instituted. For, as Martin Luther said, government is instituted in order to provide for the best interests of its subjects.

---

[28] Romans 13:1-5; 1 Peter 2:13-17.

And the Bible says a wicked ruler is as dangerous as a roaring lion or a charging bear.[29]

### 2.2 Natural law theory

Another basis for the overthrow of a government may be found in natural law theory canvassed by 17th and 18th century social contract theorists.[30] According to the Englishman, John Locke, the purpose of all government is simply to preserve the members of a given society in their lives, liberties and possessions. The power of government is conceded on trust by the people to the ruler for him to rule only for the public good. So long as government fulfils this purpose its laws should be binding and obeyed. But when government ceases to protect or begins to encroach on the natural rights to life, liberty and 'estate', the laws enacted by a government that behaves in that manner lose their validity. The mythical social contract is then automatically dissolved. The government loses its very *raison d'être* and can therefore be overthrown. The people are then free to conclude a new social contract with another ruler who will be willing to rule consistently with the terms of the contract.

Somewhat similar social contract views were propounded by the Swiss, Jean-Jacques Rousseau. According to him *la volonté générale* (the 'general will') is, by natural law, the sole and unfettered legal authority in the state. The 'general will' is the 'will' of the people taken together as a whole, constituting an entity. It is not the mere sum of the individual wills of the citizens. Any actual ruler is a ruler only by delegation of the 'general will' and could be removed whenever rejected by the 'general will'. Rousseau's doctrine implied that the people are the real rulers and they could overthrow at their discretion anyone ruling them. In this sense, Rousseau's doctrine was more revolutionary than that of Locke. It was more revolutionary because it supplied the doctrine of the sovereignty of the people, the

---

[29] Proverbs 28:15.
[30] C Anyangwe, *Introduction to Human Rights and International Humanitarian Law*, University of Zambia Press, Lusaka, 2004, pp. 12-14.

supremacy of the General Will, and the emotional spirit that makes people ready to rebel.

The English (1688), American (1776-1781), and French (1789) Revolutions were all influenced by the ideas of Locke and Rousseau. The English Revolution established the principle that a ruler could be removed by popular will if the ruler failed to observe the requirements of constitutional legitimacy. The American revolutionaries were more emphatic when they boldly declared that:

"Whenever any form of government becomes destructive ... it is the right of the people to alter or to abolish it, and to institute a new government ... most likely to affect their safety and happiness."

And that:

"When a long train of abuses and usurpations, pursuing invariably the same object evinces a design to reduce [the people] under absolute despotism, it is their right, it is their duty, to throw off such government, and to provide new guards for their future security."[31]

Almost a century later, President Abraham Lincoln concluded his short but poignant address at Gettysburg, 1863, in these words:

"It is for us the living, rather, to be dedicated here to the unfinished work that they who fought here have thus far so nobly advanced. It is rather for us to be here dedicated to the great task remaining before us that from these honoured dead we take increased devotion to that cause for which they gave the last full

---

[31] See, the Declaration of Independence of the United States of America. The document, firmly anchored in natural law theory and primarily the work of Thomas Jefferson, was adopted by the Continental Congress in Philadelphia, on 4th July 1776, and since then that date has been celebrated in the USA as the country's Independence Day.

measure of devotion – that we here highly resolve that these dead shall not have died in vain – that this nation, under God, shall have a new birth of freedom – and that *government of the people, by the people, for the people*, shall not perish from the earth."

Lincoln's concept of democracy as government of the people, by the people and for the people is arguably a refurbishment of the ideas of Locke and Rousseau. That concept of democracy implies that the governor governs only by permission of the governed and that a government which is not democratic or which ceases to be democratic may legitimately be replaced by the sovereign people. The 'American Creed' accepted by the US House of Representatives in 1918 incorporates Lincoln's concept of democracy when it recites, "I believe in the United States of America as a government of the people, by the people, for the people, whose just powers are derived from the consent of the governed."

### 2.3 *International Human rights law*

A further basis for the overthrow of government may be found in international human rights law. That law ordains that all governments derive their authority from the consent of the governed. The Universal Declaration of Human Rights declares that the "will of the people shall be the basis of the authority of government …"[32] The implication of this provision is that any government which does not rest on and enjoys popular consent may be removed. However, such removal would have to be by constitutional and democratic process since the Declaration directs that the will of the people shall be expressed in *periodic* and *genuine* elections.

In an interpretative resolution adopted in 1996 the African Commission on Human and Peoples' Rights introduced the concept of elections into Article 13 (1) of the African Charter on Human and Peoples' Rights. That sub-Article simply provides that, "Every citizen shall have the right to participate freely in the government of his

---

[32] Article 21 (3).

country, either directly or through freely chosen representatives in accordance with the provisions of the law." The interpretative resolution asserts that in terms of the Charter elections are the only means by which people can democratically choose their government.

What if the method of periodic and genuine elections is unavailable or beyond reach or made impossible? It would seem, on principle, that in such a situation the people may resort to force or to 'flash mob' or street action or any other form of popular demand for regime change such as the so-called 'yellow revolution' in Eastern Europe or the 'Arab spring' in North Africa. That would be justified on the basis of the law of internal self-determination in terms of which all *peoples* have the right to freely determine their political status and to freely pursue their economic, social and cultural development according to the policy they have freely chosen.[33]

Those who forcibly capture power can always justify their action on any of the above theoretical bases and claim to be simply an executing agency of the people, acting at their behest, on their behalf, and in their best interest. Some speak of a 'people-supported' or a 'people-accepted' take-over. It may therefore be posited that natural law theory and human rights law provide the philosophical foundation of the rise of 'people power' and the revolutionary overthrow of unwanted governments.

## Coups typologies

Coups are sometimes classified as either 'breakthrough', 'guardian', or 'veto' types. However it is classified, a coup is always premeditated and planned; it is always the result of a conspiracy by a small close-knit group within the military. Even the so-called 'spontaneous' coup is necessarily planned even though on the surface political power is seemingly thrust on a seemingly unwilling military.

---

[33] Article 1 common to the International Covenant in Civil and Political Rights and the International Covenant on Economic Social and Cultural Rights, 1966; Article 20 (1) the African Charter on Peoples' and Human Rights.

Two possible scenarios may give rise to the type of takeover sometimes described as a 'spontaneous' coup.

### 3.1 Consensual coup

Firstly, there is what might be called a 'consensual coup' or 'coup by invitation'. Such a coup is carried out with the connivance or complicity or acquiescence of the incumbent government following that government's failure to deal with a particularly acute situation in the country. This may happen when the political situation in the country deteriorates to such an extent that the established government finds it difficult or impossible to rule. The executive then 'invites' the military to take over and restore order and normalcy. Apparently the implied understanding is that after the military would have achieved its limited mandate the military interregnum comes to an end and power handed back to the democratically elected government. In such a case then, the military takes over power with the fiat of the established government and the apparent benediction of the population. This appears to be what happened in Sudan in 1958 when General Abboud took over power and in Nigeria in January 1966 when Major-General Aguiyi-Ironsi became the Nigerian military strongman following the coup led by Major Nzeogwu.

For the jurisprudent, the question that arises in this sort of situation is whether the existing constitution and legal order survive the military take-over. If the existing constitution survives then the validity of the legislative and executive acts of the military government would have to be judged by reference to it. In the Nigerian Supreme Court case of *Lakanmi & Anor v. The Attorney-General of the West* [34] learned counsel for the Appellant argued strenuously that the military takeover in Nigeria in January 1966 was by invitation of the rump of the existing government. Therefore,

---

[34] (1971) 5 *Nigerian Lawyers Quarterly* 133; N Rubin & E Cotran (ed.), *Annual Survey of African Law*, vol. 4, 1970, p. 28. For comments on that case, see DIO Eweluka, 'The Military System of Administration in Nigeria,' (1974) 10 African Law Studies at p. 75 et seq.; A Ojo, 'The Search for a Grundnorm in Nigeria – The *Lakanmi* Case,' (1971) 20 I.C.L.Q. 117.

counsel went on, there was no revolutionary takeover. The constitutional order valid until then (i.e. the 1963 Constitution) survived the takeover and continued. Consequently the military government had no power to go against the Constitution.

The learned Attorney General replied that after soldiers killed the Prime Minister and certain of his key ministerial colleagues the so-called invitation by the surviving ministers to the military to move in and save the Constitution was a mere façade. What actually took place, he submitted, was a revolutionary overthrow of the constitutional order then in existence. The constitution valid until then did not survive the coup, except in so far as some of its provisions were saved by the new government itself. The new government did not have and did not claim to have constitutional backing. It did not derive its powers from the 1963 Constitution and could not be expected to abide by its provisions. The military government may have saved certain provisions of that Constitution. But in theory of law the authority behind the saved constitutional provisions was no longer the people but the military government itself and that document cannot properly be referred to as the 1963 Constitution. The military government obtained its power by sheer force and the source of its authority is the revolution that gave birth to it. The Attorney-General then concluded that the military government was an unlimited government. It could make and unmake any law as it saw fit.

The Supreme Court was not swayed by this line of argument marshalled by the learned Attorney General on behalf of the state. It ruled that the military government was not a revolutionary government but an interim one of necessity brought in to save the 1963 Constitution and safeguard the lives and properties of citizens; and that that Constitution still subsisted as the supreme law of the land and could not therefore be violated even by the military government. The Court thus ruled in favour of the appellant. But it was a Pyrrhic victory. The military government lost no time in passing a decree nullifying the judgment and, for the avoidance of any doubt it ousted the jurisdiction of the courts from inquiring into the validity of any of its decrees or proclamations.

It must have been a surprise that the Court failed to be moved by the cogency of the argument by the learned Attorney-General. The thesis canvassed by him was indeed very compelling and ought to have prevailed. Following the elimination of the country's Prime Minister and certain of his key ministers there was no longer any proper government because there was not even an Acting Prime Minister. Even the rump of the government had ceased to function as an effective administration. Without the Prime Minister, head of government, there was no valid government left that could possibly have issued a constitutionally valid invitation to the military to take over the reins of power. But even if there was a proper government it had no power under the constitution to delegate or transfer the plenitude of governmental power to the military. The military have no business with politics. If the situation in the country had so deteriorated that the existing government was unable to deal with it the constitutional and democratic course that dictated itself was for the government to resign and call fresh elections. The sovereign people would then have elected a new government that would have had to deal with the situation at hand. This did not happen. It followed that the so-called invitation to the military to takeover was a fake or pretended invitation. What happened was indeed a military coup d'état.

### 3.2 Creeping coup

The second scenario, distinguishable from that of a 'consensual coup', is what one may call a 'creeping coup'. The situation that often gives rise to such a coup is one where there is political confusion in the country, popular discontent, popular revolt, a situation of virtual anarchy. The government seems powerless. The population is restless and appears to be inciting the soldiers to take over government. The military watches events from the side-lines (claiming neutrality) as discontent grows and revolt spreads, with the government unable or incapable of addressing the situation. At an opportune moment the military then moves in, sacks the government and takes over with the moral support and acclaim of the people who then hail the coup makers as 'liberators'. This is what happened in Ethiopia leading to the overthrow of Haile Selassie by Andom and Mengistu, in Mali leading to the overthrow of Moussa Traore by Toumani Toure, in the Congo leading to the overthrow of Lumumba by Mobutu, in Sierra Leone leading to the overthrow of Siaka Stevens by Momoh, in 2010 in Madagascar leading to the overthrow of Marc Ravalomanana by Andry Rajoelina and the military, and in the same year in Niger leading to the overthrow of Mamadou Tanja by middle level officers. In this situation the overthrow of the government inevitably entails the overthrow of the existing constitution and legal order. The revolution then secretes its own constitution and legal order.

### 3.3 Bloody and bloodless coup

In many cases the first coup or attempted coup usually involves considerable bloodshed as was the case in Cameroun, Nigeria, Ghana, Togo, and Liberia. The fighting between loyal and rebel soldiers involves heavy loss of lives and when the rebels finally gain the upper hand they proceed to assassinate the head of state and key political figures. If it is the loyal troops that eventually have the upper hand they summarily execute the rebels and those, including even civilians, suspected of having supported the rebels or applauded their action.

In some cases, the coup, usually the second or subsequent one, is relatively or even completely 'bloodless'. In all cases the successful coup is usually accompanied by the arrest of surviving members of the government and key ruling political party officials and their subsequent 'trial' (if at all) and execution or imprisonment. In that context, being a head of state or a key politician in Africa is a risky, life threatening occupation.

SOLDIERS MANNING A STREET CORNER

# Chapter 4

## How to Stage a Coup

There are available a few manuals on staging a coup d'état[35] though what applies in one country may not necessarily hold true for another. Generally, however, a coup d'état in Africa is often a simple affair given the weak institutional, legal, psychological, social and economic foundation of many states. In his book, *Dark Days in Ghana*, 1966, Nkrumah made the accurate observation that a coup in Africa is an easy thing and that all that is needed is "a small force of disciplined men to seize the key points of the capital city and to arrest the existing political leaders."

MILITARY VEHICLE BLOCKS A STREET FOLLOWING A COUP

---

[35] K Connor & D Hebditch, *How to Stage a Military Coup from Planning to Execution*, Pen & Sword Books, 2008; E Luttwak, op. cit.; JD Goodspeed, *Six Coups d'Etat*, Viking Press, New York, 1962; C Malaparte, *Techniques du Coup d'Etat*, Paris, 1931.

## Prior agreement on salient matters

The conspirators normally agree beforehand on who their leader would be and who would make the broadcast should the coup succeed. They also agree on the strategic date, day and time for their action which they usually code-name. In some cases they would choose to act when the ruler is away abroad (as in the case of Nkrumah) or away out of the capital city (as in the case of Obote). This is often the case if they assess there would be resistance from the presidential guards. By striking when the ruler is abroad or out of town the coup makers correctly reckon that any sustained resistance by the praetorian guards would be futile as the ruler would easily be prevented from getting back into the country or the capital city. In many cases however the coup makers take the ruler completely unawares in state house by using the ruler's own body guards to eliminate him if he resists arrest as in the case of Tolbert of Liberia or to take him prisoner if he offers no resistance and then to deal appropriately with him later.

## Strategic control of the capital; emergency measures

Meanwhile the armed conspirators take control of the capital city under the cover of darkness by 'capturing' strategic locations, buildings and installations: radio and television house, telecommunication installations, state house, parliament building, the international airport (usually in the capital city), and the seaport(s), if any. They put soldiers with the necessary competence and expertise to oversee radio and television, telecommunication facilities, and the airport so as to ensure that the civilians in charge of these facilities do not frustrate the coup enterprise through the use of their technical skills. Simultaneously, soldiers in armoured vehicles take up positions at strategic corners of the city while others patrol the streets, ready to neutralize any form of organized or spontaneous resistance by civilians or a non-cooperating military unit.

The tune of martial music over radio and television heralds a successful coup. The action of the coup leaders is announced over radio and television, against the backdrop of martial music. A voice comes over and announces that the ruler has been deposed and his government dismissed. As soon as the military depose the country's ruler they set about institutionalizing the new revolutionary order by adopting certain 'emergency measures.' The announcement always contains the following measures imposed by the new regime: a dusk to dawn curfew; prohibition on going into the streets under pain of being shot at sight; severing of domestic and international communication links; closure of the airport, seaport, the land borders and the airspace; suspension or abrogation of the constitution and abolition of all offices held under it (except their own of course); ban on all public meetings and demonstrations and rallies; proscription of political parties and party political activities; dismissal of the government; and dissolution of parliament.

The new regime then quickly decides the fate of the members of the overthrown government and other apologists of the regime. More often than not key regime members and apologists are arrested and summarily executed or tried by a military tribunal and then executed or imprisoned. The dissolution of parliament is however generally never followed by the arrest of all Members of Parliament, in part because the military are only too aware that many African parliaments play only a marginal, peripheral and rubber-stamp role in the governance of the state. The act proscribing or suspending other organizations such as trade and students unions provides the necessary legal pretext for persecuting their leaders and members: some are arrested and detained while others are stripped of their political rights or are banned from running for public office.

The rebel regime suspends or curtails the enjoyment of basic human rights and muzzles the press. In fact, one of the first measures taken by a military regime is control of the media. Freedom of expression and opinion is curtailed. The independent media is closed or restricted. Censorship in one form or another (official pre-censorship or self-censorship) is imposed to make sure the editorial and journalistic staff toe and stay in the official line. Any 'deviationism' becomes punishable either as 'espionage', 'defamation of head of state', 'spreading of rumours', 'propagation of false news', 'publishing alarmist news', or simply as a crime against state security.

In a military regime therefore there is very little scope for expressing opinions that conflict with those of the usurper regime. There is no scope for denouncing regime violations of human rights from within the regime. There is no scope for dissent or debate. This is one reason why a military regime is inherently undemocratic even when it is a benevolent dictatorship or even when its leaders use the language and symbolism of democracy in some of their public pronouncements.

## Judges and civil servants

When the military seize power they always never proceed against the judiciary or the civil service. But nothing stops them from arresting and executing say the chief justice or other senior member of the judiciary who in their suspect rulings were particularly zealous in defence of the regime now ousted. Generally, however, the military would be extremely foolish to move against the entire judiciary or civil service. That would be like shooting themselves in the foot. Both the judiciary and the civil service provide a measure of continuity and stability in an otherwise chaotic situation. Besides, both the judiciary and the civil service are retained by the military as legitimization symbols.

The civil service is vital for the management of the state and for ensuring administrative continuity when governments change hands. It is always left more or less intact when the military take over the executive and legislative powers of the state. If the public service were to be dismissed the military regime would be totally incapacitated and the country would cease to function. So, through legal acrobatics, by decree, public offices held under the previously existing legal order are abolished and automatically revived, explicitly or implicitly. The holders of the various offices are then deemed to hold or to act in the equivalent office under the new constitution. In that way the legal basis of offices held under the civil service are deemed derived not from the abolished constitution but from the decree promulgated by the military usurpers. The offices are not considered a continuation of the previous ones because that would mean acknowledging their prior existence. They are considered in law to have been created by the new legal order though for certain practical matters such as promotion, retirement benefits, pension etc. the computation of time would necessarily relate back to the time of initial appointment.

Generally the military also tend to leave the judiciary undisturbed.[36] This is intriguing, if not paradoxical. But it is hardly surprising when it is remembered that one of the justifications sometimes advanced for a coup is that the ousted government interfered with and subverted the judiciary. The military cannot therefore seek to interfere with or otherwise try to subjugate the judiciary. Another reason why the military often tends to observe the proprieties towards the judiciary is that the judiciary is necessary for purposes of legitimization of the new dispensation and for the peaceful settlement of day-to-day disputes among individuals. There are of course exceptions as where in Uganda Idi Amin had Chief Justice Kiwanuka executed extra-judicially.

However, the fact that members of the judiciary and of the public service are seldom dismissed does not mean that the workings of those services may not be interfered with. In a military dispensation there is nothing like a no-go area. There are no sacred cows. Military-regime interference with the courts is not uncommon. Such interference often takes the form of limiting the subject-matter jurisdiction of the courts. It is usual for a military regime to interdict the courts from pronouncing on the validity of any of the 'laws' of the usurper regime. It is also common for a military regime to issue a decree ousting the jurisdiction of the courts in certain important

---

[36] A.N.E. Amissah, 'The Role of the Judiciary in the Governmental Process: Ghana's Experience,' *African Law Studies*, No. 13, 1976, p. 4.

matters, thereby seriously disrupting the balance of power in the state and seriously compromising judicial independence. The military tend to create military or special or so-called 'revolutionary' tribunals, vesting them with wide jurisdiction and providing that their decisions are final and not subject to appeal to the ordinary courts. The proliferation of military or special tribunals under military regimes is very disturbing because these tribunals do not form part of the judiciary but come under the executive. In the military the hierarchical structure is inflexible and there is this habit of submission to those in command. It is therefore rare for military judges and prosecutors (assuming that they have the requisite training or expertise in law) to maintain the necessary independence of mind that the delicate task of administering justice requires.

The various 'emergency measures' adopted by the coup makers are of course illegal (as indeed the coup itself) under the constitution valid before the coup. The abolition of that constitution is therefore meant to remove the taint of illegality which would otherwise attach to all actions of the usurper. With the constitution abolished, the new regime becomes a law unto itself, changing its own decrees as it sees fit and exercising power beyond judicial control. Indeed the usurper regime acts very much beyond the pale of the law. So far as there is any submission at all to the rule of law by the military rulers, it is a self-denying ordinance.

## Coup by the executive

There have been cases where an incumbent government, tacitly or expressly aided and abetted by the military, assumes extra-constitutional powers, completely altering the character of the existing constitutional order and ushering in a totally different one. The incumbent government in effect overthrows the existing constitutional order and brings in a different one. This situation is sometimes denoted as a 'self-coup'. A 'self-coup' always has the tendency of breeding a rebellion in the form of a counter-coup or an insurgency leading to the ouster of the self-coup maker and the restoration of the *status quo ante*.

The very idea of the executive branch of government overthrowing the constitutional order of the state may appear far-fetched but it is real and has happened in some countries. In France, First Consul (President) Louis Napoleon Bonaparte carried out a coup d'état in 1802, dismissed the French Assembly and proclaimed himself Consul (President) for life. His new dictatorship was approved by an overwhelming plebiscite. Just two years later, in 1804, he abolished the French Republic that he headed, proclaimed the French Empire and literally crowned himself Emperor. Napoleon would later be overthrown by a coalition of European powers. The French eventually abolished the monarchy and reinstated the republic.

In Peru, President Albert Fujimori, although elected, assumed in 1992 total control of the country's legislature and judiciary in addition to the executive he already controlled. He became a totalitarian ruler in every sense of the word. Fujimori was subsequently overthrown, tried for treason, convicted and jailed. In Nepal, King Gyanendra assumed emergency powers in 2005 and became a despot. He was eventually stripped of all powers by an insurgency, the monarchy abolished and a republic proclaimed.

In Ethiopia, Emperor Haile Selassie abolished the federal arrangement between Ethiopia and Eritrea and absorbed Eritrea as part of Ethiopia. That action gave rise to the Eritrean insurgency which secured independence for Eritrea after thirty years of fighting. Haile Selassie was eventually overthrown and died held in captivity. In Nigeria, General Ironsi who had assumed power by coup d'état abolished the Nigerian Federation and decreed that country a unitary state. That action prompted a counter coup in which Ironsi was killed and the federal republic re-instated.

In Cameroon, Ahmadou Ahidjo, President of the informal Cameroon 'Federation', in violation of the constitution and his oath of office taken as federal president, abolished in 1972 the federal set up between Cameroun Republic and the former United Nations

Trust Territory of the Southern Cameroons under British Administration. He decreed a Jacobin unitary state and then formally annexed and occupied the former British Southern Cameroons as a part of his native Cameroun Republic. The federal constitutional order, including the federal and state legislatures and governments, were abolished and the Southern Cameroons state together with its Assembly and other governmental structures decreed out of existence. Ahidjo then assumed total powers in the totalitarian dispensation that he ushered in. That ill-considered action gave impetus to and intensified the Southern Cameroons self-determination struggle that is bound to come to fruition.

In the Central African Republic, Bokassa who had come to power by coup d'état, abolished the republican constitutional order, proclaimed that country an empire and crowned himself emperor. Bokassa would later be overthrown, the empire abolished and the republic reinstated. In what was then Rhodesia (now Zimbabwe), Ian Smith, the country's colonial leader representing the British Crown, unconstitutionally declared the country independent from Britain and assumed indefinite and unchecked powers. Smith's unilateral declaration of independence (UDI) at once prompted a nationalist struggle that eventually ended in independence for Zimbabwe in 1980.

King Sobhuza II of Swaziland reigned for over 60 years (1921–82). He had 70 wives, 210 children and 1000 grandchildren. Swaziland achieved independence from Britain in 1968 under his reign. Before the British left they gave the country a constitution under which the existing tribal government was changed into a constitutional monarchy. But barely five years after the Kingdom became independent, on 12 April 1973, Sobhuza abrogated the 1968 Westminster-originated Constitution. He dissolved parliament and banned political parties. He assumed full powers and instituted rule by proclamation. He thus became absolute ruler of Swaziland.

In jurisprudential terms this was a revolutionary overthrow of the constitutional order then in existence in Swaziland. Indistinguishable from a military coup in its effect, the overthrow was illegal in terms of the constitution valid until then. The success of the self-coup created its own legal order, a new legal order. Although certain provisions of the 1968 Constitution were saved, the authority behind the saved provisions was the King's Proclamation, not the abrogated constitution. The provisions rescued from the defunct constitution were incorporated into the said Proclamation by necessary intendment since they could possibly not have any independent existence. The 1968 Constitution contemplated only the possibility of 'alteration' (a terminology that presupposes survival of the constitution), not complete repeal or abrogation (which entails demise of the constitution). Since Sobhuza's action Swaziland has politically been restless. There is a continuing struggle for democracy, led by trade unions. Some in the country would want the monarchy abolished and a republic proclaimed.

Ahidjo

Selassie

Bokassa

Sobhuza II

# Chapter 5

## Coups and the International Community

The endless and widespread coups in Africa demonstrate and confirm the instability of African states and the apparent inability of Africans to govern themselves properly and democratically. At first coups in Africa appeared to have been welcomed by a large section of the international community. The West in particular saw the coup d'état as a necessary method of effecting regime change to put 'friendly' regimes in power.

### Attitude of international organizations generally

The early attitude of the United Nations and the then Organization of African Unity towards military coups in Africa reflected deficiencies in international law and internal response to coups. Both held on to outdated concepts of sovereignty. They held on to old concepts of non-interference in the internal affairs of a state. As a result they refrained from condemning military coups. What is more, the international community and international law recognized the principle of 'effective control' rather than the principle of 'genuine consent by the people' as the critical indicator of regime sovereignty and legitimacy. This meant that the international community could not discourage unconstitutional changes in government and anti-democratic behaviour in developing countries.[37] Nowadays, a noticeable change of attitude is reflected in the fact that coups in Africa are greeted with condemnations and calls for restoration of 'constitutional' government.

---

[37] C Sampford and M. Palmer, *The Theory of Collective Response*, Lexington Books, 2005. (http://www.soros.org/initiatives/washington/); A. Mindua, 'L'ONU face aux coups d'état militaries et aux gouvernements non-democratiques,' 6 *RADIC* (1994) 209.

Jurisprudence teaches that the process of law relies upon both authority and control. In the language of that law discipline, the process of law relies upon effectivity or efficaciousness. When the military take over control of a country, there is bound to be the basic question whether they had the authority to do so. Constitutionally and from a positivistic point of view they of course do not have any such right or authority. Third states and international organisations therefore appear justified in condemning coups and calling for the return to 'constitutional' government. International reaction against some coups could be swift. For example, in swift reaction to the coup in Niger in 2010, ECOWAS suspended that country's membership of that Organization and subsequently adopted sanctions against the country. The EU also suspended over US$600 million in annual budgetary support and development aid, and the US froze over US$50 million in non-humanitarian support.

The point should not escape notice, however, that established governments hate military takeovers because the action is an unconstitutional means to power and is destabilizing and inimical to peace and security. The denunciation of coups by established governments can therefore be expected. The condemnation of coups by inter-governmental organisations also comes as no surprise because these bodies are the creation of governments. The African Union, for example, is strongly opposed to unconstitutional accession to power. It considers coups a bane to democratization, good governance and development in the continent.

Coup-minded soldiers therefore face a serious dilemma. If their coup project fails they become liable to prosecution for treason. If it succeeds they and their government may find themselves under economic and military sanctions, including travel bans and asset freeze by bilateral or multilateral partners, designed to persuade them to return the country to democratic governance. Democracy demands that the military be subordinate to the civil authorities and democratic governance is now a condition for either bilateral or multilateral donor assistance.

## Attitude of Western countries generally

However, reaction to coups in Africa, especially by Western countries is not always productive. For instance, sometimes some Western countries (e.g. the United States of America, Britain and France) intervene militarily or diplomatically in Africa in the name of democracy. But in fact such intervention is done to safeguard their interests since they do not always withhold recognition of regimes that have come to power by unconstitutional means, but grant it so long as a regime is seen as 'moderate'. For instance, the US initially condemned the coup in Mauritania by Mohammed Ould Abdel Aziz against President Taya, but later recognized the junta's control. Apparently the US did so because the new regime promised to hold elections in two years and assured foreign oil companies that they will honour existing oil contracts. France adopted a similar attitude with regard to Niger, Togo, Guinea and Chad. In the recent coup of 21 March 2012 in Mali, the US and France nonchalantly called on both sides to resolve their problem through peaceful means, whatever that meant since the method of the rebel soldiers was not peaceful and the incumbent government was already overthrown. The long term effects and the perception of supporting non-elected regimes did not appear to bother the United States or France. At the end of the day it would seem third states accept or oppose a military government as their own self-interests dictate.

It seems therefore that when a Western government considers a usurper regime to be of 'moderate character' or receives assurance from it to be 'friendly' and of no threat to the Western government's interests, recognition and support would likely not be withheld. By recognising and supporting the usurper regime, the Western government sacrifices at the altar of political expediency civil and institutional organizations fighting for real change and for a democratic society. A Western government that recognises and supports the usurper regime incurs the charge of double-standard and political hypocrisy. It may be the case that some of the new military officers who come to power are genuinely committed to the welfare of their people as in the case of the Gambia. But it is necessarily the case that these officers come to power through illegitimate and unacceptable means.

The international community would have to take a principled stand in this matter. On the one hand, if the existing regime has overstayed its welcome and is corrupt, if it is dictatorial and brutal, then it becomes necessary to remove it. The soldiers who do so ought to be hailed, recognised and supported. The leaders of the ousted regime must then be tried for any alleged crimes and human rights abuses committed by them and their accomplices. On the other hand, if the ousted regime was a democratically established government and did no wrong then the usurper regime ought not to be recognised and the usurpers should be tried as soon as there is a return to constitutional rule. Supporting a legitimate government, even if it is an 'unfriendly' one, would be an effective deterrent to coups and a genuine commitment to upholding the will of the people.

## Attitude of the African Union specifically

Since 2001, whenever a military coup has taken place in Africa, the African Union (AU) reacts by issuing a statement condemning the coup and calling for return to constitutional rule. Membership of the AU may be affected by suspension. The specific powers of suspension and the circumstances in which they may be exercised are provided for in Article 30 of the Constitutive Act of the Union. The Article stipulates that "Governments which shall come to power through unconstitutional means shall not be allowed to participate in the activities of the Union." This provision clothes in treaty form a decision adopted in the Algiers Summit in 1999, and since reaffirmed on several occasions, rejecting all unconstitutional changes of government.

I have argued elsewhere that it would be too restrictive and inconsistent with the mischief which Article 30 seeks to cure to construe the expression 'unconstitutional means' as limited to 'military coups' and that acquisition or retention of political power say through election rigging or abuse of the constitution clearly comes within the term 'unconstitutional means'.[38] Furthermore, not all governments in Africa are 'constitutional' or 'democratic'. Not every government in Africa comes to power or retains power through constitutional and democracy means. Not all governments in Africa are legitimate regimes. There is no reason why such governments should enjoy treaty protection.

The AU is against unconstitutional changes of governments.[39] And whenever such a change occurs in the continent it does not hesitate to call for "the return to constitutional legality". However, the AU has never clarified what it means by that phrase. It is not clear whether the requirement of return to constitutional legality is satisfied by simply organising so-called 'free and fair' elections and handing over power to whoever wins, including the leader of the military junta who may have contested the elections. It is also not clear whether return to constitutional legality means the overthrown constitution and the ousted ruler and his government must be reinstated. The practice of the continental Organisation in this matter is of little guidance. In the case of Sierra Leone, the deposed government of President Kabba continued to be recognised as the legitimate government of that country and the military junta that had seized power was prevailed upon to hand back power to the ousted government. In other cases, for example, in Mauritania, Guinea Bissau, Central African Republic, and Togo, it was sufficient that 'elections' were organised and it did not seem to matter that the 'winner' was the very leader of the military junta that had seized power or the person on whose behalf the military had staged the coup.

---

[38] C Anyangwe, 'The Constitutive Act of the African Union,' *Zambia Law Journal*, vol. 38, 2006, p. 43.

[39] C Anyangwe, Understanding the Phenomena of Unconstitutional Changes of Government in Africa, in SBO Gutto (ed.), *Shared Values, Constitutionalism and Democracy in Africa*, Forune-Africa Publishing, Johannesburg, 2011, pp. 26-48.

Sometimes, as in the cases of Guinea, Madagascar and Niger, the AU is 'satisfied' with a mere promise by the usurper government to hold 'free and fair' elections within a couple of years or so. In the case of Mauritania, the AU did not insist on President Ould Ahmed Taya and his government being returned to power. It was the USA that initially called for "peaceful return to order under the constitution and the established government of President Taya." The EU did not go that far. It simply called for "full respect for democracy, human rights and the rule of law."

The AU threat of suspension embodied in Article 30 of its Constitutive Act has therefore not eliminated or even diminished military takeovers in Africa. Between 2000 and 2008 there were nine African coups and in 2009 alone there were four. In December 2011 there was an attempted coup in coup-prone Guinea Bissau and, two months later, there were two successful coups in quick succession, one in March and another in April 2012. In March 2012 there was coup in Mali followed shortly afterwards by the secessionist declaration of 'Azawal state' in the north of the country by Tuareg rebels.

Many of Africa's successful coups ousted undemocratic and repressive civilian regimes. Some have therefore been quick to assert that such unconstitutional actions may be an unpleasant but necessary option to remove ineffective or repressive governments, though admittedly AU documents on elections and governance seek to establish and protect constitutional rule, not effective governance *per se.*[40] Not surprisingly, many of these coups are welcomed by citizens. Intriguingly too the coup leaders enjoyed co-operation, recognition and support from regional bodies in the continent. The *Communauté Economique et Monétaire de l'Afrique Centrale* (CEMAC) gave Bozizé of Central African Republic a red-carpet treatment after he ousted elected leader Ange Patassé. The Economic Community of West African States (ECOWAS) pushed for the departure of

---

[40] I Souare, *The AU and the Challenge of Unconstitutional Changes of Government in Africa,'* Institute for Security Studies, 2009. http://www.iss.co.za/dynamic/administration/.

democratically elected Charles Taylor from Liberia and negotiated the 'resignation' from power of Kumba Yaya in Guinea-Bissau.

The reason for this seeming ambivalence is simple. The AU and the rest of the international community make uncritical and blanket condemnations of coups. They call for the reinstatement of the former government. But these pronouncements sometimes stand in stark contrast to the wishes of the people of the coup country. In a number of cases the people do publicly welcome a coup. By that public support for the coup the people are clearly sending across the message that they do not desire a return to the former so-called 'constitutional government' and its so-called 'rule of law'. Where a regime or government has become despotic and no longer serves the needs and interests of the people, a change, whether brought about by military or insurgency takeover, is likely to be supported by the people, though sometimes the new dispensation turns out to be just as despotic and corrupt as the old one.

Most African leaders have been in power for decades, in some cases for virtually as long as the continent was formally decolonised. They make a mockery of the electoral process, muzzle opposition and turn their countries into personal fiefdoms. They send dissenting voices either into forced exile or to jail or to the other world. In some countries corruption is pervasive and the leader is usually richer than the state, displaying sinful opulence and affluence while the majority continues to wallow in abject poverty and squalor. This sorry state of political disorder associated with governance in African has always been an excellent recipe for military intervention and accounts for the growing number of military coups in the continent.

The logic is simple. Those who make peaceful change impossible make violent change inevitable. When it becomes impossible for a people to change through the ballot box an unwanted regime they turn to the military. They look up to the soldiers to effect regime change in the hope of a future improvement in their wretched lot. They even look up to an outside power for deliverance, especially in circumstances where the military is suspected to be in cahoots with the hated and despised despotic government.

Nowadays, each coup in Africa is followed by calls from the international community for a return to the rule of law and constitutional order. But one cannot credibly talk of a *return* to the rule of law and to constitutional order where in the coup country, the rule of law and constitutional order were never experienced in the first place; where the ousted government was itself not a constitutional government at all and the rule of law was completely absent. It is for this reason, I would submit, that these days there are no longer calls for power to be returned to the ousted government. Calls that are made are for early free and fair elections to be held and a return to civilian rule.

At the end of an AU summit in January-February 2010 AU leaders, in a flight of unrealistic ambition, expressed in a resolution, their determination to put an end to military coups in Africa.[41] But in 2009 alone, four military coups were recorded in various parts of the continent. There have been other coups or coup attempts since the January 2010, the most recent coup being the one in Mali in March 2012. Clearly it would take more than mere fine resolutions to end the coup syndrome in Africa. It is doubtful that the best antidote to coups could be found in fine rhetoric or fantastic resolutions. Some commentators believe that the best antidote to coups is to be found in good governance and leadership that is accountable and incorruptible; in an electoral system that is free and fair and respects the true wishes of the people in its outcome; in openness and true respect for the rights and privileges of the citizenry and the provisions of the sanctity of the constitution; and in the use of available resources for the greatest happiness and welfare of the majority.

---

[41] http://allafrica.com/africa

THE AU, UN, AND EU FLAGS

# Chapter 6

## *Grundnorm* and Revolutionary Legality

A revolution occurs when there is an overthrow of an established government by those who were previously subject to it, or when there is a forcible substitution of a new ruler or form of government. In other words, there is a successful revolt or rebellion against the *status quo*. A coup d'état is thus a revolution although it does not often result in a dislocation within the country as always happens in the case of a classic revolution. However, when analysed from the jurisprudential point of view, the effect of a military coup is the same as that of a classic revolution.

The effect of a coup or a revolution depends on whether it fails or it succeeds. If a coup fails, the attempt is interpreted as an illegal act, as the crime of treason. The attempted coup-makers become rebels and liable to imprisonment for treason under the legal order they attempted to overthrow. The coup having failed, the existing legal order remains intact; the existing constitution remains and the *status quo* continues. But if the coup succeeds the existing constitution, in fact, the entire legal order, is radically altered; it is swept away; it is overthrown. The constitution valid until then is replaced with other laws promulgated by the revolutionaries. There is an enforced fresh beginning. The old order changes, yielding place to the new. The success of a revolution thus results in a new *grundnorm* being presupposed or established.

### Grundnorm and the hierarchy of norms

The question is: when does a coup succeed? The eminent legal philosopher, Hans Kelsen[42] says it succeeds when it is efficacious. By

---

[42] An Austrian-American, Hans Kelsen (1881-1973) was the exponent of the positivist pure theory of law. He expounded that theory in his classic work, *The Pure*

'efficacious' he means two conjunctional requirements: (i) that the coup is generally accepted by the people *and* (ii) that the laws of the coup makers are obeyed by the people and enforced by the courts. The learned jurist argues that if the revolutionaries succeed, if the old order ceases, and the new order begins to be efficacious, because the individuals whose behaviour the new order regulates actually behave, by and large, in conformity with the new order, then this order is considered as a valid order. It is now according to this new order that the actual behaviour of individuals now has to be interpreted as being legal or illegal.

Source: http://shikelgruber.net/sitebuilder/images/kelsen-14

*Theory of Law,* written in 1934 at the age of 54, thirty-eight years before his death at 92. Kelsen believes the phenomenon of law should be studied and analyzed in isolation, free from other social science disciplines. His pure theory of law endeavours to free the science of law from all foreign elements. Kelsen's position thus differs from the one taken by other jurisprudents who argue that law cannot usefully be studied and analyzed isolated from related disciplines such as sociology, economics, history, anthropological, psychology, and so on, an opposing view pushed even further by two iconoclastic juristic movements, Realism and Postmodernism.

In his seminal work, *General Theory of Law and State*, Kelsen analyses how a legal system works. In it he adumbrates the theory that is now generally referred to as the *hierarchy of norms*. Kelsen sees law as essentially a normative science; that is to say, a science of norms; a norm being a legal rule of human conduct. For him, law operates as a hierarchy of norms; that is, a series of legal rules set out at various levels of generality and subordination. The highest norm is the most general and therefore the most abstract. Norms of a lower level are increasingly concrete in their form and application. By this process of concretization norms become more and more specific.

In the hierarchy of norms each norm derives its validity from the valid norm one step before it. What this means is that the validity of a norm depends upon whether it was made in terms of a higher valid norm. Kelsen posits that the law regulates its own creation. In other words, the creation of legal norms is authorized by other higher valid legal norms. Every legal norm is validated by another prior valid norm higher in the hierarchy of norms. These norms can be traced back to the highest norm in the hierarchy of norms. They can be traced to an initial norm denoted by Kelsen as the *grundnorm,* that is to say, the basic norm.

The *grundnorm* is therefore the starting point of the chain of legal norms. It is at the apex of the hierarchy of legal norms. It is the original source of authorization for the decisions and actions taken throughout the system, down to its lowest level. For as long as there is continuity in the existing legal order, for as long as there is no revolution such that there is a change or a break in the legal order, the *grundnorm* does not change.

The constitution of a state is itself a norm and being a norm it is validated by another prior valid norm higher in the hierarchy of norms. The constitution is not the *grundnorm.* The *grundnorm* operates from a higher point, that is, one step further back. It gives validity to the constitution-making process and to the constitution that is the outcome of that process. In turn the constitution gives validity to the next norm immediately below it (legislation by parliament), which likewise gives validity to the next norm immediately below it (statutory instruments), etc. Since the grundnorm is at the highest level of abstraction the closer a norm is to the *grundnorm*, the more abstract it is; the further away it is, the more concrete it is, the lowest norm being the most concrete.

Kelsen's jurisprudential system is thus a legal system consisting of hierarchically arranged legal rules, all of which have the *grundnorm* as their one ultimate source. The entire body of law appears as a pyramid of laws. At the apex of the pyramid is the *grundnorm* and at the base are the lowest norms. Scholarship is unanimous that Kelsen's jurisprudential theory is analytically excellent and that its logicality is not easily assailed.

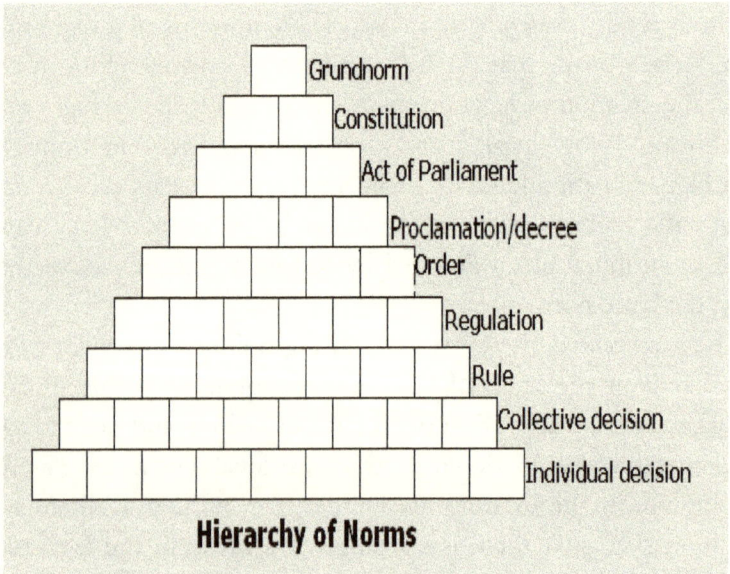

**Hierarchy of Norms**

## Grudnorm and coup d'état

Kelsen posits that the effect of a coup is the complete destruction of the *grundnorm* of the previously existing legal order. The validity of the new *grundnorm* depends on its efficacy. That efficacy itself depends on whether the constitution put in place by the usurper is obeyed by the people and enforced by the courts. If the people disobey the new constitution put in place by the usurper regime, if the courts decline to enforce the new constitution, then the new *grundnorm* is inefficacious and the revolution would then have failed. But if the new constitution that is put in place is obeyed by the people and is enforced by the courts, then the new *grundnorm* is efficacious. The revolution succeeds. The revolutionary change resulting from the revolution takes effect.

The revolutionary change does not however mean a change in *all* the laws of the previous regime. It is common for the main body of the old laws to continue unchanged. It is thus not the entire legal order that is changed or swept away. For example, there may be no loss of continuity in the civil and criminal law after a coup d'état. However, what does change completely is the *grundnorm*. The grundnorm of the previous legal order is destroyed and a new *grundnorm* is presupposed. Laws of the old order that are not revoked by the new regime are deemed impliedly decreed into existence. Such laws are deemed validated by the usurper regime and so remain valid within the framework of the new order. Accordingly, the saved old-order laws have to be obeyed just like the new laws that are expressly decreed by the regime. This is how Kelsen captures this idea in *General Theory of Law and State*:

"From a juristic point of view, the decisive criterion of a revolution is that the order in force is overthrown and replaced by a new order in a way which the former had not itself anticipated. Usually, the new men whom a revolution brings to power annul only the constitution and certain laws of paramount political significance, putting other norms in their place. A great part of the old legal order 'remains' valid also within the frame of the new order. But the phrase 'they remain valid' does not give an adequate description of the phenomenon. It is only the content of these laws that remain the same, not the reason of their validity. They are no longer valid by virtue of having been created in the way the old constitution prescribed. That constitution is no longer in force; it is replaced by a new constitution which is not the result of a constitutional alteration of the former. If laws which were introduced under the old constitution 'continue to be valid' under the new constitution, this is possible only because validity has expressly or tacitly been vested in them by the new constitution. ... The laws which, in the ordinary inaccurate parlance, continue to be valid are, from a juristic viewpoint, new laws whose import coincides with that of the old laws. ... Thus it is never the constitution merely but always the entire legal order that is changed by a revolution. This shows that all norms of the old order have been deprived of their validity by revolution and not according to the principle of legitimacy. And they have been so deprived not only *de facto* but also *de jure*. No jurist would maintain that even after a successful revolution the old constitution and the laws based thereupon remain in force, on the ground that they have not been nullified in a manner anticipated by the old order itself. Every jurist will presume that the old order to which no political reality any longer corresponds has ceased to be valid, and all norms, which are valid within the new order, receive their validity exclusively from the new constitution. It follows that from this juristic point of view, the norms of the old order can no longer be recognized as valid norms."

The new constitution that is put in place following the coup d'état, derives its validity not from some other norm but from the coup itself. The coup or revolution is a momentous historical event. It is a factual situation having the power to create new law. The coup or revolution is then the *grundnorm*, the basic norm. Kelsen's *grundnorm* theory is thus the foundation of his thesis that when a successful revolution occurs, the *grundnorm* of the old legal order is destroyed and there is established a new *grundnorm*, the validity of which depends on its efficacy. The revolution is thus at once both a destructive and a creative event; destroying the old and establishing a new *grundnorm*.

# Hierarchy of norms and revolutionary destruction of the grundnorm

The relationship between the principle of hierarchy of norms and the doctrine of the revolutionary destruction of the *grundnorm* is this. The *grundnorm* is the substratum, the foundation of the pyramidal legal edifice now inverted so that it stands on its head. With the pyramid inverted, the *grundnorm* is now at the base. The structure now looks like an improper fraction; it is an inverted collapsible pyramid. The *grundnorm* is now the foundation carrying all the norms in the legal system.

A coup d'état, a revolution, has the effect of destroying this base or foundation on which all the norms of the entire legal system are anchored and linked, and from which they derive their validity. That destruction results in the crumbling of the collapsible pyramidal legal structure, meaning that the entire legal system inevitably collapses. The destruction of the *grundnorm* automatically sets a chain reaction in motion. The immediate norm standing on the destroyed *grundnorm* crumbles. Likewise, the immediate norm standing on the crumbled norm also crumbles. This chain reaction is repeated with respect to all successive norms in the legal order. All these norms come crashing down like a house of cards.

"A legal system is thus like an inverted collapsible pyramid with the *grundnorm* as the foundation rock. The *grundnorm* is the ultimate norm from which all subordinate norms in the legal system derive their validity. If one takes away the *grundnorm,* then the inverted pyramid collapses for lack of support. Since Kelsen believes that the effect of a coup d'état is the destruction of the *grundnorm*, this means that, in his eyes, the legal effect of a coup d'état is to remove the bottom rock of the collapsible inverted pyramid and thus to send the whole structure crashing down." [43]

---

[43] SK Date-Bah, 'Jurisprudence's Day in Court in Ghana', *International and Comparative Law Quarterly, V*ol. 20, 1971 at p.317.

```
                                    Individual decision
                                  Collective decision
                               Rule
                             Regulation
                           Order
                         Proclamation/decree
                       Act of Parliament
                     Constitution
                   Grundnorm
```

**Inverted Collapsible Pyramid**

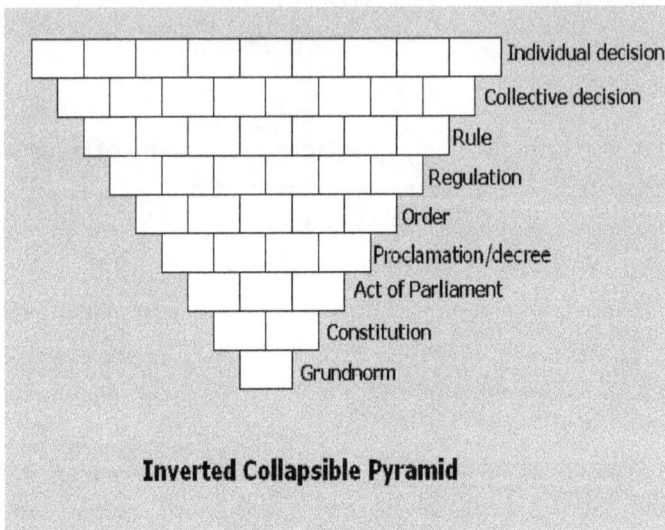

### Further explication of the meaning of grundnorm

Kelsen reasons that the *grundnorm* is the 'initial hypothesis' that validates and authorizes the creation of all legal rules. He posits that one cannot account for the validity of the *grundnorm* by pointing to another rule of law. For him, since the *grundnorm* is not traceable to any other norm, its validity is presumed and this must be so as long as the norms constituting the legal order remain effective.

So what then is the *grundnorm*? Kelsen informs us that it is the '*basic norm*' of a legal order, that is, the norm forming the base or foundation of the legal order. Kelsen reasons that the *grundnorm* is the last presupposition, the final postulate, upon which the validity of all the norms of the legal order depends, including the validity of the constitution that is the first historically. This means when one starts from the norm at the lowest level of the pyramid of norms and moves upwards one eventually gets to the highest norm on top of the pyramid. This is the ultimate norm. There is no other norm higher than this one since there can be no norm higher than the highest norm. This norm is the *grundnorm* because the validity of all other norms underneath depends on and derives their validity from it.

Speaking in linear terms one would say the *grundnorm* is the initial or foundational norm for other norms and beyond which there is no other norm. It is the alpha norm, so to speak. In normative terms the *grundnorm* is the equivalent of God in Christian epistemology. God is the creator of everything. He is the alpha. Beyond Him there is nothing else. Likewise, the *grundnorm* is the originating source of all other norms. Beyond the *grundnorm* there is no other norm. The *grundnorm* itself is necessarily valid because otherwise there would be nothing like a legal act. Kelsen maintains that the basic norm is presupposed to be a valid norm. He reasons that it is so presupposed because without this pre-supposition, no human act could be interpreted as a legal act, especially as a norm-creating act.

The *grundnorm* is thus not the same thing as the constitution which, being itself a norm, necessarily derives its validity from some other norm higher than itself. The *grundnorm* is a presupposition of the validity of the constitution or the legitimacy of a ruler. The history of a people is the foundation or source of its legal system. This history is prior to any contemporary legal system. Whatever legal system is in existence is traceable from the history of that society. This history is presupposed to have law-creating powers and is therefore the *grundnorm*. It is from this foundation that a society's values which are contained in a constitution are drawn. Whenever there is a major fission in the historical continuity of a society's social and legal order the force or phenomenon (the revolution) that unleashes the fundamental change and thus discontinuity, becomes a law-creating force. A new *grundnorm* is then presupposed.

For example, before independence, a colonial legal order obtained in dependent territories. That legal order came to an end with the demise of colonial rule. The elimination of colonial rule through consensual or forcible decolonization was a revolution which brought about a new social, political and legal order. This new revolutionary order brought with it the Independence Constitution. The Independence Constitution is the first constitution historically, deriving its validity from the revolutionary new social, political and legal order which came into being after colonialism had been done away with. Some colonial laws usually survive the revolutionary new order. But the authority behind the saved colonial laws is no longer the departed colonial power but the revolution, the law-creating phenomenon that eliminated colonial rule. In simplistic terms, that revolution is the *grundnorm*. This *grundnorm*, the new revolutionary historical process, gives birth to and validates the new constitution.

Take South Africa for example. The apartheid legal order that existed in that country came to an end with the demise of apartheid. The defeat of apartheid was a revolution which brought about a new social, political and legal order, and a democratic dispensation underpinned by a new Constitution deriving its validity from that revolutionary new order. The new *grundnorm* that conferred law-creating powers to the framers of the 'historically first constitution' of the new South Africa is the historical process that brought about the defeat of apartheid and gave legal validity to the 1994 interim and then the 1996 final Constitution. The validity on which the historically first constitution rests is merely the pre-supposition that the new document ought to be obeyed. The validity of that new document does not rest on the fact that it was framed by eminent lawyers and politicians. Nor does it rest on the fact that it was adopted by "we, the people of South Africa ... through our freely elected representatives". The mode of adoption of the new document is only a procedural matter.

The *grundnorm* authorizes the ruler, the historically first legislator, and prescribes that one ought to behave as the framers of that constitution ordain. The whole function of the *grundnorm* is to confer law-creating power on the act of the first legislator and on all the other acts based on the first act. A country's initial constitution, deriving its validity from the *grundnorm*, may undergo a number of constitutional amendments and revisions, but not revolutionary discontinuity. Should revolutionary discontinuity occur, as happens when there is a coup d'état, a new *grundnorm* will be established. The *grundnorm* is thus the starting point of the constitutional order when there is a political *tabula rasa* or an enforced fresh beginning of a revolutionary overthrow of a constitutional order.

## Possibility of legal void following a coup

The sociological jurist would concede that Kelsen's analysis is logically sound as far as its internal consistency is concerned. But he would argue that the analysis could be socially undesirable in that it is capable of resulting in the creation of a period of legal void when a country's government is overthrown.

A legal vacuum may arise when there is an interval between a coup entailing the destruction of the existing constitution, and the moment when a new constitution is instituted by the coup makers. If the entire pre-existing constitution and laws automatically cease to be valid at the time of the successful coup with no continuity at all of legal systems there could be inconvenient legal hiatuses of lawlessness before a new constitution is put in place. Similarly, if the old *grundnorm* is destroyed and the new one that is presupposed is not valid until it is efficacious, there could be a gap of legal uncertainty and lawlessness. That is a consequence which is socially undesirable.

Therefore, the sociological jurisprudent would submit that certain laws in a legal system ought to survive the destruction of the *grundnorm* of that system.[44] While this argument is persuasive it must be remembered that the surviving laws would now have to be tested by reference to the new constitution (deriving its validity from the coup) that is eventually put in place by the new government. That could present some challenges. Still, this problem points to the inconvenience, at least in the African context, of Kelsen's theory of the effect of a coup being the destruction of the entire legal order of a state, creating a legal *tabula rasa*. It is significant that African coup makers never renounce their military ranks and privileges conferred upon them under the previous legal order.

---

[44] SK Date-Bah, op.cit. p.315.

## Authority and legitimacy of the usurper government

When a coup is successfully carried out the military government assumes effective control of the country. But being in effective control is one thing and having authority to act is another thing. The usurper government has authority only if the people yield obedience to its commands. If the usurper government is without authority its directives and proclamations would lack the character of law. However, if the people, generally, show their support for the new government and obey its commands and the commands are enforced by the courts, the new government acquires both authority and legitimacy retrospectively from the inception of the coup. The coup, the revolution, succeeds because it has the weight of the people behind it.

Since the revolution has the weight of the people behind it, the dignity and peace of the people of the coup country require that the legality and legitimacy of the new and successful revolutionary government be not impugned whether by municipal courts, by third states, or by international organisations. So long as the people demonstrably want the new government and support it, how that government initially came to power and the fact that it did not come to power in accordance with the rule of law, would seem to be of no moment.[45]

The problem however is determining the degree of support that the new government would have to enjoy for one to say it has the weight of the people behind it. What indicators would suggest that the usurper government enjoys popular support? What degree of popular support is required? This point of uncertainty is another reason why Kelsen's theory of revolutionary legality may not be adequate in the African coup context. For example, a few or even all of the people in the capital city or even rented crowds may come out into the streets rejoicing at the overthrow of the old regime. But it

---

[45] OH Blayton, 'African Coup d'etat: the sequel – and the rule of law', 28 December 2008: http://www.africaloft.com

would be doubtful if that would be sufficient indication that the people of the country are generally in favour of the coup.

## International law and recognition of the usurper government

Internally, the success of a coup or putsch entails its 'acceptance' by acquiescence. Internationally, it entails the *de facto* or *de jure* recognition of the new government by other governments. International law is indifferent when it comes to the internal legitimacy or legality of a government. At international law, a state has a discretionary power to recognize or not to recognize another state or a foreign government. Beyond that, the international community will deal with whatever government is in effective control over any country. According to the weight of contemporary international law juristic opinion, recognition is cognitive, not constitutive.

The fact that third states recognize a government at their discretion does not however mean that states and inter-governmental organizations have adopted the principle of non-interference in its absolute sense. The AU Constitutive Act, for example, declares in Article 30 that "Governments which shall come to power through unconstitutional means shall not be allowed to participate in the activities of the Union." This provision is interpreted as also requiring African States not to recognize any African government that has come to power by unconstitutional means. The prohibition contained in Article 2 (7) of the Charter of the United Nations precludes the Organization from intervening in matters which are "essentially within the domestic jurisdiction" of a state. The phraseology of that provision suggests that intervention is permissible in two situations: in matters that are *not* within the domestic jurisdiction of a state, and in matters which though within its domestic jurisdiction are not *essentially* so. Such intervention would be justifiable either under the doctrine of humanitarian intervention or in the interest of international peace and security.

The UN Charter does not in express terms prohibit coups. But from the spirit of that document it is legitimate to conclude that coups are impliedly prohibited. The agenda set by the Charter includes the promotion of peace, stability, security, freedom and development. The purposes and principles of the United Nations are, inter alia, the development of friendly relations among nations based on respect for the principle of equal rights and self-determination of peoples, and the achievement of international cooperation in promoting and encouraging respect for human rights and for fundamental freedoms for all. What may also be extracted from this is that the exigency of democratic legitimacy is binding on states as a matter of both internal and external self-determination.[46]

There appears to be a number of factors pointing to an emerging principle of democratic legitimacy in international law. First, regimes based on racialism and oppression, such as the then apartheid regime in South Africa and the racist regime of Ian Smith in Rhodesia, were condemned, sanctioned and ostracized from the international community. Second, international law appears to have a predilection for democratic political regimes as expressive of the will of the people, which will is the basis for all state authority. International law does not turn a blind eye to an external oppressor; it is doubtful that it should turn a blind eye to an internal oppressor. Coups are inherently anti-democratic and coup makers are, by their disposition and mind set, tyrants. Acceding to power by sheer use of arms is contempt of the people and a criminal abuse of the instruments of force put into the hands of soldiers by the taxpayer.

## National constitution and military coup

Theoretically a military coup could be constitutional in the sense that it occurs within the framework of the existing constitution; in other words, the constitution, most unlikely, provides for a coup as a

---

[46] Cf. TM Franck, 'The Emerging Right to Democratic Governance,' *AJIL*, 1992, vol. 86, 56; DW Bowett, 'Self-Determination and political rights in the developing countries,' *ASIL Proceedings*, 1966, p. 133.

valid method of acceding to power. In such an unlikely event, the constitution is then the source of the authority of the military government that has seized power, survives the coup, and limits the powers of the new government. Since the change of government is effected under and within the existing constitution, the new government has a direct and unbroken link with it.

Where the constitution permits regime change through coup d'état and the military seize power in fulfilment of the wishes of the sovereign people to uphold the constitution, the military government that is formed would not be a usurper government; it would not be a revolutionary government; it would be a constitutional interim government. Under such circumstances the constitution survives and the powers of the military government are strictly limited by the constitution which it can neither offend nor amend except to the extent demanded by necessity.[47] It is however trite observation that the army never comes to power under a constitution because forcible capture of power has never been and is not a valid constitutional method of acceding to power.

A tricky situation arises where, after a coup, the military regime decrees the *suspension* of only certain provisions of the constitution rather than the suspension or abrogation of the entire document. In such a case the regime may properly be taken as intimating that the coup was carried out within the framework of the existing constitutional order and that the constitution survives. But where the soldiers who seize power declare the existing constitution repealed or overthrown, then that constitution ceases to exist and therefore cannot be suspended because there is nothing to suspend; the constitution no longer exists and cannot therefore be suspended. The usurper military government cannot be taken to have declared the suspension of the provisions of a dead and ineffective constitution. A dead constitution can only be revived, wholly or in part. By contrast,

---

[47] *Lakanmi & Kikelomo Ola v.The Attorney General of Western Nigeria,* (1971) 5 Nigerian Lawyers Quarterly 133. "A revolution occurs," said the court in that case, "only where there is a disruption of the constitution and the national legal order by an abrupt political change not contemplated by the constitution."

when a democratic change of power takes place the constitution survives the change; what falls or is overthrown or ousted is the government of the day and not the constitution.

Can the 'voluntary' handover of power by the civil government to the military be reasonably read into a constitution, even in circumstances of necessity or circumstances of emergency? One hastens to wonder why a civilian government would hand over power to the military rather than go to the country. The power to handover to the military cannot be read into the constitution unless there is an express constitutional provision that clearly authorizes a hand-over. The power to hand-over cannot be implied unless it is so closely and directly connected with some express power that the two must be taken to have been jointly granted by the constitution. In other words, the power to be implied as incidental must be a necessary preliminary to, or an unavoidable corollary of, an express power.

There must be a main power for there to be an incidental power. The operation and the extent of the incidental power will then depend upon the exercise and existence of the main power. The power to uphold, execute and maintain a constitution does not included an implied power to liquidate the government and the authorities it established. It is doubtful to the extreme that the power to execute and maintain a constitution implies the power to abdicate and surrender the constitution and its administrative institutions to the military.

More usually, a military coup is a revolution in the sense that the military dislodge and displace the incumbent government in a manner not contemplated or sanctioned by the existing constitution. In that case the constitution is overthrown and cannot therefore be the source of the authority of the military government. The military regime has no direct link with the constitution. It is not bound or limited by it. There is a break with the past legal order. It follows that where there is a forcible overthrow of a government, the succeeding government owes its position not to a pre-existing legal order, but to the events that toppled the immediately preceding administration. The forcible overthrow marks an end of a legal order and the beginning of a new one. The coup effectively abrogates the whole pre-existing legal order except such as is saved and preserved by the succeeding administration.

A coup is a revolution, which is the accession to power by extra-constitutional means. The military obtain power by sheer force or threat of it. They do not obtain power under the constitution since the coup is not just the overthrowing of the government but also of the constitution itself. The military government formed after the coup cannot therefore claim to have any constitutional backing; and it cannot be expected to abide by or respect the provisions of an overthrown, inexistent, constitution. Even where, following a coup, the constitution is saved by the military government the authority behind the saved constitution is no longer the sovereign people but the military government which in turn derives its authority from the coup, the revolution, that gave birth to it.

What this means is that the military regime is an unlimited government domestically. As an incidence of its legislative omnipotence it can make and unmake any law on any subject whatsoever in the country. It also has executive omnipotence and so is the supreme and unlimited policy making authority in the country.[48] Externally, however, the military government remains subject to international law and must respect obligations arising from treaties and other sources of international law and international responsibility incurred by the ousted government. Thus it was held in the Nigerian Court of Appeal case of *Fawehinmi v. Abacha*[49] that:

> "While the Decrees of the Federal Military Government may override other municipal laws, they cannot oust the jurisdiction of the Court whenever properly called upon to do so in relation to matters pertaining to human rights under the African Charter. They are protected by the International Law and the Federal

---

[48] DIO Eweluka, 'The Military System of Administration in Nigeria,' *African Law Studies*, No. 10, 1974, p. 72.

[49] (1998) 1 HRLRA 541, per Musdapha J at p. 590.

Military Government is not legally permitted to legislate out of its obligations."

SOLDIERS CLASH WITH CIVILIANS FOLLOWING A COUP

# Chapter 7

## Usurper Government: its Legitimacy and the Validity of its Acts

Coups in Africa are revolutions inside sovereign states with two possible situations. The usual situation is that in which the coup results in the complete disappearance overnight of the old regime and constitutional order. When that happens, the possibility of the courts continuing to operate in terms of the authority of the previous order also disappears.

The other situation is that in which there is simply a change of personnel at the top layers of the government without any major changes in the constitution or its laws, although the authority behind them has changed. In this situation the old order survives and continues to function by permission of the new order. Members of the judiciary then suppose that they are acting strictly legally in continuing in office and applying the norms of the new effective regime.

### Judges and the overthrow of government

Whenever a revolutionary overthrow of an established government takes place judges invariably find themselves caught up in the rebellion in the sense of being confronted with two hard and unpleasant alternatives. The judge could resist the new regime and hinder the growth of its power by resigning his appointment in the hope that the normal functioning of the courts would be paralyzed. Alternatively he could stay on in office and either co-operate with the new regime by carrying out its commands, thereby legitimizing it; or temporize by adopting a wait-and-see attitude in the hope that domestic and international pressures on the usurper regime will force it to collapse.

## 1.1 Resignation

Indeed, judges could, acting individually or collectively, signify disapprove and rejection of the military seizure of power by resigning their judicial appointments on conscientious grounds in the hope of paralyzing the judicial system and thereby helping to bring down the usurper government. If the judges collectively resign they would be making a statement that the regime is not legitimate and that its acts are not valid. Apart from the Rhodesian UDI situation in which two judges resigned their judicial appointment on conscientious grounds[50], judges hardly resign their appointments even in a coup situation. Therefore the proposition that all the judges could resign must be a mere theoretical and far-fetched one. It is not a practical proposition even in the context of a small judiciary. It is even more remote in the case of a large and dependent judiciary, such as one finds in most African countries. At any rate, it is doubtful that it is part of the duty of a judge to assist in dislodging the usurper government or to assist it in maintaining itself in power.

In many African countries, a judge who decides to resign may be taking a serious personal risk. In some countries collective resignation by judges or individual resignation of a judge in pursuance of a common purpose may be construed as subversion or treason and punished as such. In any case, it does not seem that resignation could ever be effectual. It is unlikely to change anything. The usurper regime is unlikely to hesitate in summarily dismissing judges who resign and then replacing them with even low calibre but compliant judges in sympathy with the usurper regime. No usurper regime abandons the power it has seized because of the moral scruples of judges. There is an even more compelling reason why the usurpers will not do so. If they were to give up the power they seized that would mean the coup has failed, and that could lay them open to prosecution and imprisonment or even execution for treason.

---

[50] The two judges were Mr. Justice Fieldsend and Mr. Justice Young.

## 1.2 *Continuation in office*

Rather than resign their offices, judges may decide to continue in office arguing that their decision to stay on is with reference to their public obligations and duties as judicial officers appointed and sworn to uphold the law and legality. If judges decide to continue in office they might sooner or later be required, in a case brought before them, to pronounce themselves on the legitimacy of the usurper regime or on the validity of its acts. At that point they must take a stand for or against the new order. If they co-operate with the new regime they would thereby have joined the revolution and so abet an illegality. By applying the enactments of the usurper regime they in fact assist its efficacy. Obedience and enforcement of the enactments of the revolutionary regime are indicia of the regime's effectiveness and the efficaciousness of its laws. The usurper's decrees are thus validated and the regime legitimized. And, if the commands of the usurper regime happen to be morally reprehensible, the judge who carries them out also violates his own conscience.

In the circumstances it seems the judge, sitting under the power of a usurper regime, has no choice but to accept the regime as legal and apply its enactments. Well might they apply the enactments of the usurper regime since their duty is to apply the law as it is, and not the law as it was or the law as it ought to be. Besides, no revolutionary regime has ever surrendered its newly won power for the sake of a judge's unhappy conscience. It might well therefore be that if judges stay in office they should recognize the new reality and give effect to the acts of the usurper regime. This is an easy option. But it is one based on realism or pragmatism. After all, by accepting judicial appointment under the usurper regime the judge by necessarily implication recognizes its authority, affirms its existence and recognizes its acts and decrees.

The court cannot legally undo the fact of usurpation. Lawful or unlawful, the existence of the usurper government is a fact, and that fact cannot be altered by the courts or destroyed by any judicial concept the judge might wish to have recourse to. This is the position African judiciaries appear to take, as can be seen in the Ugandan case of *Uganda v. Commissioner of Prisons, Exparte Matovu.*[51] In that case the court in Uganda upheld the validity of the overthrow of the Constitution by Milton Obote, the country's Prime Minister. The court based its decision on the Pakistani case of *The State v. Dosso*[52] in which the Supreme Court applied Kelsen's theory that if a revolution is effective it creates its own legal order. The Court ruled that a change is in law a revolution if it annuls the Constitution and the annulment is effective.

"If the attempt to break the Constitution fails, those who sponsor or organize it are adjudged by the existing Constitution as guilty of the crime of treason. But if the revolution is victorious in the sense that the persons assuming power ... can successfully require the inhabitants of the country to conform to the new regime, then the revolution itself has become a law-creating fact because thereafter its own legality is judged not by reference to the annulled Constitution but by reference to its own success."

In its ruling in *Uganda v. Commissioner of Prisons, Exparte Matovu* the High Court of Uganda accepted the correctness of this approach. The approach was also accepted by the High Court in *Lardner-Burke v. Madzimbamuto*[53] and other Rhodesia UDI cases decided both in Rhodesia and in London in the Judicial Committee of the Privy Council.[54]

---

[51] (1966) EA 514.

[52] Pakistan Law Digest 1958 SC 533.

[53] [1968] 2 S.A.L.R. 284 (Rhodesia); for other judicial acceptance of Kelsen's doctrine of revolutionary legality, see *Makotso & Ors v. King Moshoeshoe II & Ors* (1988) Lesotho unreported civil judgment; *Sallah v. The Attorney General for Ghana* (1970) Current Cases; *Valabhazi v. Controller of Taxes* (1981) Seychelles Civil Appeal, unreported; *Mitchell v. DPP* [1985] LRC (Const.) 127 (Grenada); *Asma Jilani v. The Government of Punjab & Anor*, Pakistan Law Digest 1972 SC 139.

[54] C Palley, 'The Judicial Process: UDI and the Southern Rhodesian Judiciary,' (1967) 30 *Mod. L. R.* 263; HR Hahlo, 'The Privy Council and the "Gentle Revolution",' (1969) 86 *S.A.L.J.* 419; RS Welsh, 'The Constitutional Case in Southern Rhodesia,' (1967) 83 *L. Q. R.* 64; TC Hopton, 'Grundnorm and Constitution: The Legitimacy of Politics,' (1978) 24 *McGill L. J.* 72; LJ Macfarlane, 'Pronouncing on Rebellion: The Rhodesian Courts and UDI,' *Public Law* (12) 1969, p. 324; A Wharam, 'Treason in Rhodesia,' *Camb. L. J.*, 1967, p. 189; RWM Dias, 'The UDI Case: The Grundnorm in Travail,' *Camb. L. J.*, 1967, p. 5.

If, contrariwise, the judges decline to recognize the legality and legitimacy of the usurper regime they will perforce not be prepared to give effect to any of its acts or measures. Should the usurper government require them to take an oath of allegiance to its constitution, the judges would decline to do so. By thus refusing to co-operate with the usurper regime the judges put themselves in a dangerous situation. They may be sacked or even murdered. Their judgment may be nullified by decree. In Nigeria when the court ruled against the military government in the *Lakanmi* case, the government swiftly reacted by promulgating a decree nullifying the judgment.

In May 2009 the Madagascar Supreme Court ruled that the street-cum-military-assisted take-over of power in the country by the Mayor of the capital city was unconstitutional and the regime illegal. The usurper regime simply ignored the ruling. In Fiji, the State President, acting on behalf of the Prime Minister, a soldier who came to power through a coup, simply dismissed the judges who had dared to suggest that the usurper regime was illegitimate. The President then simply appointed new and compliant judges. In Niger, President Tanja who had come to power through a coup d'état tried to stage-manage a 'referendum' that would remove presidential term limits and so virtually making him life president. But the country's Constitutional Court thrice ruled that any such referendum would be unconstitutional. Tandja reacted by simply dissolving the Court, claiming it lacked the competence to judge such matters.

No usurper regime has ever had difficulties replacing unaccommodating, reactionary judges with compliant ones. There is also another reality. It is very doubtful that judges could decide to continue in office and realistically refuse to cooperate with the usurper government. An implication of the judges' continuation in office is their reliance on the new regime for payment of judicial salaries, for the provision of facilities for the day-to-day working of the courts, and for the execution of court judgments. Execution of court judgments would necessarily involve giving legal effect to some at least of the legislative and executive acts of the usurper regime.

Overall, it seems wholly unrealistic for judges to continue in office and yet refuse to cooperate with the usurper regime in a situation where the usurpers are in effective control of the executive and legislative arms of government. If the judges continue in office but refuse to uphold the usurper's laws then they would have worked themselves out of their jobs because they cannot uphold the laws of the predecessor regime as those laws have been decreed out of existence by the usurper regime.

SCALE OF JUSTICE; COMMON LAW/CIVIL LAW JUDICIAL OUTFIT

### Legitimacy of the usurper government

The concept of the legitimacy of governments has philosophical, legal and political dimensions. A government can be legitimate in accordance with the constitution of the country. It might even be recognized as legitimate by the international community. However, the citizenry might not deem it so if the government has ceased to be responsive to their aspirations. Rules or practices of international law cannot decide the internal legitimacy or otherwise of the government of a state. That is a matter for the municipal law applicable in that state. Recognition at international law rests on political discretion based on the reaction of a foreign state to a new regime.

Legitimacy under municipal law is something else. Its essence is captured by the American Declaration of Independence in these ringing words:

"… whenever any Form of Government becomes destructive … it is the Right of the People to alter or to abolish it, and to institute a new Government, laying its foundation on such principles, and organizing its powers in such form, as to them shall seem most likely to affect their Safety and Happiness. … When a long train of abuses and usurpations, pursuing invariably the same Object evinces a design to reduce them under absolute Despotism, it is their right, it is their duty, to throw off such Government, and to provide new Guards for their future security."

So if a government is unresponsive to the needs, wellbeing and wishes of the people, it loses its legitimacy in their eyes and may righteously be abolished by them and a new one instituted in its place.

# *De jure* status of the usurper regime: the doctrine of effectiveness

When a revolution takes place it may be, and often takes, a while before any issue of legitimacy is raised in court. Sometimes the issue arises only when the usurper regime has ceased to exist. When the issue does arise the court would then have to determine whether to accord the usurper government *de facto* or *de jure* status. It seems that in municipal law, a government has *de jure* status if it is one which *ought* to possess the powers of sovereignty; it is the rightful, lawful government "though at the time it is deprived of it".[55] In international law a regime's *de jure* status is sometimes founded on the doctrine of effectiveness, that is to say, on the regime's firm and effective control over the country, such that there is a complete replacement of the old order by the new.

The doctrine of effectiveness as a *conditio sine qua non* of the validity of acts promulgated by the usurper regime is authoritatively propounded in Kelsen's *General Theory of Law and State*. From what Kelsen posits, it appears that the internal success of a revolution is all that is required for the validity of the acts of the new regime. Kelsen argues that:

> "The norms of the old order are regarded as devoid of validity because the old constitution and, therefore, the legal norms based on this constitution, the old legal order as a whole, has lost its efficacy; because the actual behaviour of men does no longer conform to this old legal order. Every single norm loses its validity when the total legal order to which it belongs loses its efficacy as a whole. The efficacy of the entire legal order is a necessary condition for the validity of every single norm of the order. A *conditio sine qua non*, but *not a conditio per quam*. The efficacy of the total legal order is a

---

[55] Cf. per Bankes L.J. in *Aksionairenoye Obschestvo, A.M. Luther v. James Sagor & Company* [1921] 3 K.B. 532 at p. 543.

condition, not the reason for the validity of its constituent norms. These norms are valid not because the total order is efficacious, but because they are created in a constitutional way. They are valid, however, only on the condition that the total order is efficacious; they cease to be valid, not only when they are annulled in a constitutional way, but also when the total order ceases to be efficacious. It cannot be maintained that, legally, men have to behave in conformity with a certain norm, if the total legal order, of which that norm is an integral part, has lost its efficacy. The principle of legitimacy is restricted by the principle of effectiveness."[56]

A criticism of Kelsen's doctrine of effectiveness is that it makes no distinction between *de facto* and *de jure* authority and that it uses as its criterion of efficacy the test whether individuals actually do behave in accordance with the new order.[57] The doctrine,

"does not require positive acceptance of the new order or even rejection of the old, simply that men no longer act in accordance with old norms which have not been "received" into the new. What is not clear is whether the Kelsen doctrine should be taken as simply a descriptive account of how men behave when a successful revolution takes place or whether it is to be read as providing an authoritative prescription which not merely justifies but requires obedience to the new regime. ... It is one thing to argue, as Kelsen does above, that men cannot be required to act in conformity with norms of a total legal order which has passed away; quite another to conclude ... that this

---

[56] This passage is taken from excerpts of Kelsen's works reproduced in MDA Freeman, *Lloyd's Introduction to Jurisprudence*, (7th ed) Sweet & Maxwell, London, 2001, pp. 287-288.
[57] LJ Macfarlane, 'Pronouncing on Rebellion: the Rhodesian Courts and U.D.I.' p. 324 at p. 334

requires that the courts of the old order are required to validate the norms of its effective replacement."[58]

The court may determine that the new regime has *de jure* status. In other words, the court rules that the regime has indeed established a new legal order and so is effectively in charge of the country. If the court so decides, it must transfer its allegiance to the regime and give full effect to all the acts valid within the new order. It must decline to formally pronounce on the regime's constitutionality.

Some writers have in fact argued that it is not the proper scope of the judicial function for the courts to determine the legitimacy or not of a government. They maintain that the issue is purely political and not legal and so beyond cognizance by the courts. In America this is categorized as a 'political question' and there has long since arisen in that country a doctrine that courts may not embark upon an inquiry into any such question.[59] The first important case in that country to apply the doctrine of judicial non-intervention in political questions was *Luther v. Borden*.

"Beginning with this decision, the idea was developed that there are some cases of which the courts are not authorized to take jurisdiction ... There are certain cases which are completely without the sphere of judicial interference. They are called, for historical reasons, 'political questions'. To what matters does the term apply? It applies to all those matters of which the court, at a given time, will be of the opinion that it will be impolitic or inexpedient to take jurisdiction. Sometimes this idea of inexpediency will result from the fear of the vastness of the consequences that a decision on the merits might entail. Sometimes it will result from the feeling that the court is

---

[58] Ibid, pp. 334, 335.
[59] *Luther v. Borden,* 7 Howard 1 (1848); MF Weston, 'Political Questions,' (1925) 38 H.L.R. 296; G Sawer, 'Political Questions,' (1963) 15 *U. of Toronto L.J.* 49; BO Nwabueze, *Judicialism in Commonwealth Africa*, Hurst & Co., London, 1977, p. 30 et seq.

incompetent to deal with the particular type of question involved. Sometimes it will be induced by the feeling that the matter is 'too high' for the courts. But always there will be a weighing of considerations in the scale of political wisdom."[60]

### De facto status of the usurper regime: the doctrine salus populi suprema lex

In municipal law a government has *de facto* status if it is actually in possession of powers of sovereignty (i.e. effectively in control of the country) but the possession is wrongful or precarious. A determination by the court that the usurper government is illegal and therefore a mere *de facto* government does not mean that on that count all its acts are necessarily invalid and may not be legally enforced and obeyed. Some acts of such a government are capable of being given binding effect.

The doctrine of state (or public) necessity (*salus populi suprema lex*) is often invoked as the theoretical basis for giving some acts of the usurper regime binding force. For example measures necessary for normal administration, and acts necessary to peace and good order among citizens are always given binding effect. Necessity is also invoked to prevent a vacuum in the law throughout the period of usurpation when the usurper regime enjoys only *de facto* status, that is, the period when the usurper government is considered unlawful as happened in Sierra Leone with Captain Koromah's military government following the overthrow President Kabba in 1997. By drawing from the doctrine of state necessity the courts in effect hold that the coup notwithstanding, the existing constitutional order subsists at least in some respects and continues. This was the basis of

---

[60] M Finkelstein, 'Judicial self-limitation,' 37 Harv. L. Rev. 338 (1923), p. 344.

the decision in *Lakanmi,* some Pakistan cases[61] and in at least one Cypriot case[62].

The doctrine of state necessity may be traced to this oft-quoted passage in Hugo Grotius' great work, *De Jure Belli ac Pacis* (The Law of War and Peace):

> "It remains to speak of the usurper of power, not after he has acquired a right through long possession or contract, but while the basis of possession remains unlawful. Now while such a usurper is in possession, the acts of government which he performs may have a binding force, arising not from a right possessed by him, for no such right exists, but from the fact that the one to whom the sovereignty actually belongs, whether people, or king, or senate, would prefer that measures promulgated by him should meanwhile have the force of law, in order to avoid the utter confusion which would result from the subversion of laws and suppression of the courts. ... In the case of measures promulgated by the usurper which are not so essential, and which have as their purpose to establish him in his unlawful possession, obedience is not to be rendered unless obedience would involve grave danger."[63]

Grotius distinguished between two types of measures promulgated by the usurper. First, there are measures which the rightful sovereign would prefer that they should *meanwhile* have the force of law, that is, acts which have the implied mandate or order of the rightful sovereign. Those measures have binding force and are enforceable by the courts, provided the rightful sovereign does not object; but if he does they are not binding and therefore not enforceable. Second, there are measures which are not essential but

---

[61] Special Reference No. 1 of 1955, PLD 1955 F.C. 435; Bengum Nusrat Bhutto v. Federation of Pakistan, PLD 1977 SC 657; Z.A. Bhutto v. The State, PLD 1978 SC 40.
[62] Att-Gen. v. Mustafa Ibrahim (1964) Cyprus L. R. 195.
[63] Quoted in Macfarlane, op. cit., p. 349.

93

aimed at consolidating the usurper's unlawful control, that is, acts intrinsically illegal or offensive. These measures are invalid and should be rejected by the courts. However, if an individual finds that disobedience of these measures would involve personal grave danger, then the measures may be grudgingly obeyed. This rider to the plea of necessity does not invalidate the doctrine *per se*. What it invalidates is the application of necessity

> "to areas and instances where the [usurper] government's necessity to act [i.e. adopting measures designed to promote and consolidate his unlawful control] arises directly out of its having created such a necessity for itself by its initial action of rebellion. ... [T]he doctrine of necessity cannot be applied in conditions of usurpation in such a way as to support the usurper against the lawful sovereign seeking a restoration of his rightful position or in the exercise of his rightful powers." [64]

---

[64] Macfarlane, op. cit. p. 350

# Chapter 8

## Facing the Coup Challenge in Africa

### What to do about coups

Coups in Africa were at first thought to be a product of the colonial heritage or the result of military training or indoctrination by former colonial powers. This thinking was informed by the fact that early coups in Africa were carried out by soldiers trained in the military academies of Western powers: Sandhurst in Britain, West Point in the United States of America, and Saint Cyr in France. It was therefore easy to blame these military training schools for infecting the African soldier with the coup virus.

"It seems that African armies modelled on the armies of Western Europe are particularly prone to attempting military coups. Perhaps armies of this type are unsuitable for African conditions." [65]

But independent African states quickly established their own military schools and for many decades now African soldiers are home trained. And yet coups are still well and alive in Africa. African soldiers are still in the thriving business of coup making.

What must therefore be done about the coup in the African body politic, assuming coups are a bad thing and should be got rid of? Proscribing coups under positive law has not prevented military takeovers. Merely writing a 'coup clause' in a constitution does not guarantee much unless accompanied by a variety of other measures.

Perhaps coups should be integrated in the basic concepts and principles of constitutional theory. Coups are no longer unusual in Africa. They have become the 'normal' way for the transfer and exercise of power. [66] They now constitute a well-established state

---

[65] Mazrui & Tidy, op. cit. p. 257.
[66] Y Ghai, 'Coups and Constitutional Doctrines: The Role of Courts,' (1987) 58 (3) *Political Quarterly* 308.

practice that could probably well be regarded as having crystallized into custom and forming part of the customary international law of the African region. Constitutional theory cannot disregard them. It cannot insist on maintaining its own ordered coherence and treat coups as a mere pathology. The challenge for African students of constitutional law is to formulate a constitutional theory that integrates coups into its basic concepts and principles.

One could set objective criteria under which a coup would be constitutionally permissible for the purpose of removing an unwanted government and allowing the early institution of another one through democratic processes. For example, provision could be made for lawful military intervention in any of the following circumstances: where an incumbent ruler rigs an election to stay in power or eliminates presidential term limits in a shameless attempt to institute a life presidency; where there is reliably attested systemic corruption; where there is gross and reliably attested repression; where an autocratic or totalitarian form of government has been instituted; where the government is incapable or unable to carry out development projects or to provide basic necessities such as water, electricity, sanitation, roads, schools and health facilities; where there is denial of basic human rights; or where there has been instituted or there is an attempt to institute an oligarchic or a hereditary succession at the helm of the state.

Military intervention under any of these circumstances is the more necessary because in all but a few African countries the people are not able to change unwanted governments. Such controlled military intervention would be a significant contribution to constitutional development, democracy and good governance in Africa. It will eliminate unprincipled coups d'état in the continent. It will project the military as guardian of the general wellbeing of the people and significantly improve the governance of Africa.

This bold proposal of course has a number of loose ends particularly relating to procedure. Listing circumstances which would invite military intervention is the easy part. But who will trigger that intervention, the military itself? What kind of evidence will be sufficient proof of the existence of any of the enumerated circumstances and who will assess the standard and cogency of such evidence? What if the military fails to act even in the face of compelling evidence of the existence of any of the stated circumstances? These are hard questions. But they can be resolved creatively.

For example, in Niger the Court ruled that the elimination of presidential term limits was unconstitutional. The ruling was disregarded. The call by political parties for military invention was in part based on this ruling and the military eventually gave ear and intervened. One can therefore provide that the military could act on its own initiative or on the request of political parties, civil society (trade unions, human rights organizations and other NGOs, students unions, women's organizations, and professional organizations), a third of the membership of parliament, or the masses in revolt against the existing dispensation. It must be presumed that any of these constituencies will not lightly call for military intervention and that there would be a credible basis for any such call. More often than not the bad governance situation would be so glaring that it speaks for itself. If the military fails to act it would have failed in its constitutional duties and the people must then resort to the 'Arab spring'-type of demonstrations until the regime collapses.

Now, Western states appear to keep the military as far away from politics as possible by insisting on an apolitical professional military. Left-leaning countries tend to deploy political commissars in military units to foster ruling party membership, particularly at key command and staff levels. In some countries parliamentary seats are allocated to the military. In other countries still, such as Egypt, the military has simply been civilianised. Some countries have experimented with militarization of all able bodied citizens, while some others have allowed soldiers to run for political office and for militarily trained civilians to be appointed to military commands.

# What to do with Africa's military

What should be done with Africa's military? Some have advocated the detribalization of the military, the improvement of the conditions of service of the lower ranks of the military, and professionalization by keeping soldiers fully occupied not with the art of war but with making a contribution to national development (a development-oriented rather than a violence-oriented army). Bolder suggestions include disarming, neutralizing, or downsizing the military.

On one view the military should simply be disbanded. Examples of such actions are not lacking. Tanzania disbanded its colonially-inherited army, Costa Rica disbanded its Army, Kenya dissolved its Air Force[67], and Cameroun disbanded its *Garde Republicaine*. After all, no African state really has an external enemy and if any one country were to be attacked by another the international community could be trusted to intervene as it did when Kuwait was attacked by Iraq. The international community will legally do so under the collective security system of the United Nations. A regional organization may legally do so under the regional collective security arrangement. International law outlaws aggression. It prohibits the use of force in inter-state relations.[68] Given these considerations, there is probably no need for standing armies in Africa. Total demilitarization removes the possibility of one African state attacking another. Admittedly that would leave the several African states at the mercy of any non-African state minded to attack it.

But even with an army every African country is at the mercy of an outside power. When France attacked Côte d'Ivoire and destroyed *in situ* its entire air force that country was helpless and the rest of Africa looked on in total powerlessness. When the US under

---

[67] '145 were Killed in Kenyan Uprising,' *The New York Times*, 11 August 1982; 'Kenya Disbands the Air Force after Coup Bid,' *The New York Times*, 22 August 1982; http://www.nation.co.ke/News

[68] C Anyangwe, 'The Invasion of Iraq: Challenge to the Charter Prohibition of Violence in Inter-State Relations,' *Journal of Juridical Sciences*, vol. 2, 2003.

President Reagan bombed Libya that country was completely helpless. When the US attacked Somalia or bombed Sudan both countries were completely helpless. When France, seemingly with the fiat of the UN, bombed Côte d'Ivoire's State House and smoked 'President' Gbagbo out of the underground bunker beneath State House where he was hiding, Africa looked on in bemused helplessness. In February 2011 the oppressed people of Libya finally revolted against Gaddafi's 42-year despotic rule. In an act of sheer madness Gaddafi decided to use war planes and heavy artillery against his own people for daring to rise up against him. Hundreds were massacred and the country was systematically being destroyed. The UN decided to intervene on humanitarian grounds and mandated NATO "to protect civilians" by destroying Gaddafi's war machine. It took months for NATO to bomb the Gaddafi regime into utter defeat. Gaddafi was killed in the process. Africa could do no more than cry pathetically that NATO had exceeded its UN mandate. A UN team of investigators was unable to determine who actually fired the shot that killed Gaddafi.

Realistically, as these examples and others show, no African army can successfully defend the state against a determined external enemy. Idi Amin's army, so victorious against unarmed civilians, could not defend Uganda against a Tanzanian army that invaded the country from November 1978 to April 1979 with the set and successful goal of removing Amin from power. Biya's army, so brave against unarmed civilians, could not dislodge Nigerian forces from the Bakassi Peninsula. The Somali army so brave in trying to Islamize all and sundry could not stop the invasion of that country by an Ethiopian army backed by the Americans. The Congolese army so ruthless against its own people could not stop the Rwandese or Ugandan invasion and occupation of parts of the Congo. The Chadian army so able in fighting civil wars could not stop the Libyan army from invading the country and occupying the Aouzou Strip.

There is thus no need for soldiers in Africa. This is the more so as most African regimes use soldiers more for internal policing, repression, and for propping up unpopular and despotic regimes. In any event, the military drain a huge part of the national budget with nothing tangible to show in return. What every African state needs is a large, well trained, and well equipped police service to effectively fight crime, arrest criminals, keep the peace, and perform ceremonial roles such as mounting a guard of honour for dignitaries, playing drums and sounding bugles at various ceremonies.

On another view the military should not be disbanded but simply down-sized to the barest minimum and with basic equipment to deal with armed criminality, to raise the alarm and temporarily hold the frontline pending assistance from a friendly power in the event of an external attack, to deal with any internal insurgency, to undertake surveillance missions, and to perform state ceremonial functions.

Still another view is that coups should be criminalized (they already are), this time by elevating it from a municipal law offence to an international crime; a species of terrorism and therefore a crime against humanity. The international community can easily reach consensus on this. By classifying a coup (plot, attempt or successful) as an act of terrorism the international community by necessary implication also denies recognition to any government that comes to power by force (as happened to the military government formed by Johnny Paul Koromah after he overthrew President Kabba). This could usefully be followed up by a United Nations Security Council Resolution adopting measures against coup plotters and leaders of attempted or successful coups. The measures could include: making them amenable before the International Criminal Court, refusal by states to grant them asylum, enforcement against them of targeted economic sanctions, travel ban against them, and freezing of their accounts abroad.[69]

Further, the state security infrastructure may somehow be integrated into the international system[70] by way of defence pacts with a foreign power (as former French colonies have done with France) or a regional military security system (similar to NATO,

---

[69] N Omoigui, 'Preventing Coups in Nigeria – Part I,' http://www.gamji.com/nowa/nowa21.htm
[70] Idem.

erstwhile Warsaw Pact, and the ECOMOG experiment in Sierra Leone and Liberia). In that way, making a coup becomes practically impossible without a major international implication. Sometimes an African state has intervened in a neighbouring country and pre-empted or crushed a coup or a military unrest: in April 1964, Nigeria intervened in Tanzania to prop up Julius Nyerere after a mutiny; Libya intervened in the Central African Republic; Senegal intervened to crush the police coup against Dawda Jawara; South Africa intervene in Lesotho.

However, defence arrangements between Francophone states and France have failed to inoculate those countries against coups. Conceivably, the AU could insure African governments against coup under its peace and security arrangements. But this can only happen if the Organization is given the right, the power and the means to intervene in any African country in the event of a coup, something African rulers, many of who have come to power through a coup, are unlikely to accept.

Some African regimes, highly distrustful of the military, have sought to insure themselves against the high risk of a coup by outsourcing security to an external security outfit. In the Comoros, Abdallah's government contracted security to Bob Denard's mercenary outfit; and in Cameroun Paul Biya's 30-year regime contracted presidential security to an Israeli outfit. Arrangements of this type are obviously not popular and tend to be regarded by the country's military and even the police as highly provocative.

Another view is that in order to counter the enduring military threat to civilian power, the gun should not be made the monopoly of soldiers. There should be a people's armed militia, ready to confront the military in any coup attempt or to join forces with the military in beating back an internal or external armed aggression. This view was strongly advocated by Franz Fanon in his *The Wretched of the Earth* written at the beginning of the independence era in Africa. Fanon cautioned that an autonomous military, "finding itself idle and without any definite mission will go into politics and threaten the government." He argued that the only way to avoid this menace was "to nationalize" the military, by which expression he meant "to educate [it] politically" and increase the militia so that in case of war "it is the whole nation which fights and works."

A people's militia certainly reduces the monopoly of soldiers over the instruments of terror within the state. The US Constitution simply gives citizens the unfettered right to keep and bear arms. "A well-regulated militia, being necessary to the security of a free state, the right of the people to keep and bear arms, shall not be infringed." (Amendment II of the US Constitution)

Sékou Touré and Julius Nyerere established a people's militia in their respective countries. This is how they did it.

"Few African governments have even attempted to transform the army into an instrument of national development or to build up a people's militia. Fewer still have had much success... Two new African states which inherited Western-style armies have managed to transform their military institutions in a way which has strengthened instead of threatening the civilian regime. These are Guinea ... and Tanzania. In 1966 Sekou Touré's government in Guinea took a decision to create civic brigades and a popular militia. ... The civic brigades were to be composed of 100 to 150 members, aged between 17 and 30, with one brigade for each district. About 8000 were recruited into the militia, whose developmental functions were defined as:

'the protection of the national frontiers, of the big economic installations, the security of the towns, ports, airports, banks, radio, petrol reservoirs and other points of strategic importance, etc., patrols of public morality in the towns, struggle against black-marketeers, prostitution and economic fraud.' The Guinea ... militia proved itself during the 1970 invasion and abortive coup attempted by Guinean exiles in alliance with Portuguese colonialists and foreign mercenaries. ... Guinea's militia is complementary to a 13,000-strong army, which has not been left in its original Western pattern but has also been integrated with the civilian leadership. There are party committees in the army as well as the militia, and soldiers can apply for admission to civil posts, and vice versa. In Tanzania, the impetus to reconsider the country's military organization, which was originally based on that of Britain, came from the humiliation of the army mutiny of 1964 ... After the 1964 mutiny, Nyerere distrusted the inherited British principle that an army must be politically 'neutral' within the domestic system.[71]

Nyerere integrated the army with the party and bought into the idea of a developmental militia by creating the national service as a countervailing force to the military. He stressed that the basis of the defence and security of the country was the people themselves. He directed the party to control the military and to ensure that the primary task of the military during peacetime was to enable the people to defend their independence and their policies of socialism and self-reliance. In order to ensure that this was effective he combined this with countrywide militia training. Army personnel were dispersed throughout the country and provided with small arms to train the militia. A national service was introduced for primary and secondary school leavers and eventually for university graduates.

Some warned the government of the dangers of arming people indiscriminately. Others thought this entire project was a sheer waste of time and manpower. But the whole project was wholeheartedly embraced by the people.[72] In that way Nyerere broke the soldiers' monopoly of military skills in Tanzania. He used various methods to popularise the military. These included the use of political ideology, training of the militia, national service, and development projects.

---

[71] Mazrui & Tidy, op. cit. pp. 257-258. During that army mutiny Nyerere had to go into hiding. He invited British troops to disarm the mutineers. In taking another look at the country's military, Nyerere took two matters into account: the danger of military anomie, as the soldiers become restless in the barracks in the face of functional redundancy; and the interconnected problem of providing a countervailing force to the military, should the soldiers be tempted to challenge civilian supremacy.

[72] Lupogo H, 'Civil-Military Relations and Political Stability in Tanzania,' (2001) 10 (1) *African Security Review* 33.

The people of Tanzania were made to understand that the defence of the nation was the duty of every citizen when called upon to do so and that the military was only the vanguard in that national endeavour.

The idea of a people's militia has failed to catch on. One reason is that the model of a people's army or militia, which is a 'penetration' model, entails "not only the explicit and formal subordination of the military to the party and government but also the politicisation of the armed forces through the inculcation of party ideology."[73] A people's army completely removes the boundaries between political authority and the military. Military recruitment is undertaken through the party and party leaders undergo military training.[74] This is likely to work only in a one-party context. So, most African countries have rather established either a paramilitary force or special armed units that are quasi-autonomous (Praetorian guards, special intervention brigades, presidential security unit etc.) as counter-weight to the mainstream military.

---

[73] M Baregu, 'Parliamentary Oversight of Defence and Security in Tanzania's Multiparty Parliament,' (2004) *Guarding the Guardians* 33, 39 http://www.iss.co.za/pubs/Books/guardiansaug04/Baregu.pdf (26/11/2011)
[74] Ibid.

SOLDIERS MANHANDLE CIVILIANS

## What to do with Africa's despotic executives

What should be done with Africa's authoritarian executives and the enduring danger of executive coups? Suggestions that have been made include: curtailment of the powers of the executive; promotion of a culture of respect for human rights, democracy and good governance; expansion of domestic political participation; giving the people a sense of control over their destiny; acceptance of the fact that the village is the unit of political action in Africa; and the decentralization of the sources of political power and legitimacy in the country.[75]

---

[75] Omoigui, op. cit.

AFRICAN LEADERS AT AU SUMMIT

## Coup counter-measures

General Ibrahim Babangida, a former Nigeria coup leader and military ruler, once thought he had found a prescription against coups. He proposed that when MPs hear martial music they should at once repair to Parliament, occupy it and resist the coup with their lives, if need be. This is unworkable. Before airing martial music the coup makers would already have secured key institutions and strategic places, sealed off street corners, and imposed a dusk to dawn curfew. Under the circumstances there is no way MPs can gain ingress into Parliament building. Even if they did, nothing prevents the military from storming Parliament Building and smoking out the MPs *à la* Boris Yeltsin in Moscow (during the failed coup attempt, known as the *August Putsch*, in 1991). In any event it is not possible for MPs to rush to Parliament building upon hearing martial. MPs do not report for work on a daily basis like civil servants do. Most MPs reside out of the seat of Parliament, some requiring a day or two to get there from their constituencies. So the 'occupation of parliament' proposal as a counter-measure against an announced coup is a bad and impracticable prescription.

The Congolese once thought they had also found the antidote for coups. They wrote into their constitution that it was the duty of every citizen to rise up against any attempted or successful coup. That too is unworkable. The stakes are heavily tilted against empty-handed civilians who have nothing with which to counter determined coup makers armed with weapons of death and mass destruction. Many armies in Africa have never hesitated to mow down hundreds of defenceless citizens as the recent examples in Cameroun (2008), Guinea (2009), and Libya (2011) demonstrate. The soldiers always do so with impunity knowing that even the international community will not go beyond the ritualistic 'condemnation' of their action.

Proposed realistic solutions to coups include: good leadership and governance; limitation of presidential and parliamentary office to one 6-year term, devolution of power to sub-national entities; and demystification of the capital city. Coups are easy in Africa because it suffices for a group of determined soldiers merely to take control of the capital city and the nation's strategic installations and institutions located there. The job is made easier because of the concentration in the capital not only of all state institutions but also of all development and most of the military and its hardware. The Praetorian Guard, always the best equipped section of the military, is in the capital and once it has been roped into a coup conspiracy or overwhelmed by the rebellious forces, bringing the coup to fruition becomes a child's play.

Other possible counter coup measures include civil service non-cooperation with the usurper regime. This however requires some individuals to organize a general strike by public servants and prevent blacklegs from moving in. This strategy was tried in Benin but it failed; it however succeeded in Egypt, Tunisia, Libya, Syria, Georgia, and in the Ukraine which witnessed public demonstration of mass popular discontent though not in the context of a coup but in that of a regime the people wanted out of office.

## Case for coups

It is possible to make a strong case in favour of the military overthrow of a government. A coup can be conceived as a remedial operation. It is the proper remedy for a diseased body politic. It is beneficent. Power in Africa tends to be corrupt, authoritarian, despotic, and held for too long. Many Presidents royalize the republic. They are noted for conspicuous consumption, extravagant life style and palatial accommodation. They tinker with the national constitution at their whims and caprices. They create life presidencies, thereby in effect converting the republic into a monarchy. They scheme on oligarchic succession. They scheme on hereditary succession by a son. They reject free and fair elections. They reject democracy. They make little distinction between their purse and the national purse. They give short shrift to the interest of the people. They preside over rotten and corrupt regimes. They make a mockery of the people and of national institutions.

Under such circumstances only the military stand between despotism and plunder on the one hand, and liberty and democracy on the other hand. Military intervention for the common good must therefore be welcome under such circumstances. Such intervention is consistent with the mandate of the military. The mandate of the military is to save the nation from the external enemy. But that mandate necessarily includes saving the nation from the internal enemy, the internal predator, the bandit government. A coup is a matter essentially within the domestic jurisdiction of a state and so neither another state nor an international organization may interfere. The African politician's fear of military intervention is the beginning of wisdom.

A coup is often carried out because the ousted ruler was corrupt, a dictator, refused to hold free and fair elections, and put beyond reach any lawful means of the people bringing about regime change. The coup is therefore carried out in order to give back to the people their liberty, their citizenship, and full control of those who govern them. That was the justification given for the coup in Mali against

Modibo Keita. Those who stage a coup under such circumstances and out of such laudable motives are hailed by the people as saviours. But such popular approval only means approval of the overthrow of the oppressor and the tainted legal order on which the tyranny drew its diseased life blood.

Approval of the dislodging of the autocratic old regime does not however mean an unconditional acceptance of the military regime that has just seized power. Free and fair elections must then be organized within the shortest possible time, say between six to twelve months, and power handed to a democratically elected government. Only then would the usurpers be justified in pleading *state necessity* as what prompted the coup which, *ex hypothesis*, is anti-democratic. The internally and internationally delinquent character of their conduct is then effaced retrospectively and they automatically get amnesty on account of their laudable conduct in the interest of the nation.

The coup leader may then, if he wishes, and as a full and equal citizen, submit himself to elections; provided he fulfils the stipulated legally valid conditions for running for public office. If he wins honestly and fairly, he becomes the new ruler but must next submit himself to the verdict of the ballot box and quit at the end of his presidential term limit, however good he might be. This scenario, which is the best for Africa, is a rare phenomenon on the continent. The closest examples that come to mind are Ahmadou Toumani Troare's coup in Mali against Moussa Traore and Jerry Rawlings' coup in Ghana against Acheampong.

For some observers, therefore, a coup is something good in that it brings about regime change and reform, and gives birth to a new order in which the country is saved from itself or from the decadence and frivolity of the politicians.[76] From the perspective of ordinary people however, a coup d'état could be the phenomenon that brings about uncertain expectations - the prelude to hope or to disaster.[77]

---

[76] G Ferguson, *Coup d'etat: A Practical Manual*, Arms & Armour Press, New York, 1987, pp 17-18.
[77] E Luttwak, op. cit.; SP Huntington, op. cit.

## Case against coups

The case against military overthrow of government is equally compelling. From time immemorial the military has always been subject to the civil order. Things must stay that way otherwise there would be a confusion of roles in the state and questions of good governance would be thrown to the dogs. Politics is a civil and not a military matter. The vocation of the military is defence not politics. If soldiers want to enter politics they are welcome. But they must first shed their military fatigues before entering the political arena. They cannot seek to gain political power through the back door, which is what they do when they shoot their way through to power.

Using the gun to accede to power is tantamount to terrorizing the people. It is terrorism because the soldiers are in effect issuing the following terroristic command to the politicians in power: 'political power or your life!' Such a command is not different from that of the bandit who holds a gun to a person's head and bellows: 'your purse or your life!' That is why the mention of the word 'coup d'état' often tends to be met with stares of bewilderment, fear, anger, or even panic.

Any contest for power between civilians and soldiers would necessarily be an uneven one; one in which soldiers are assured of victory even before the contest begins because soldiers monopolize the state's instrument of coercive power, of terror. A military government always seeks to legitimize its coup by organizing a sham election in which the coup leader is the sole candidate. Sometimes the coup leader accepts other candidates but then intimidates them so that they pull out of the race or, if they do not pull out, he simply rigs the elections and proclaims himself winner. In some cases, the coup leader simply ignores calls for elections, declares himself a civilian and stays in power for as long as he chooses to or until mercifully removed by another coup.

The track record of soldiers who have acceded to power is nothing to write home about. Therefore, soldiers have no moral right to pontificate about lack of democracy, accountability and good

110

governance in civilian dispensations in Africa. Some of Africa's worst rulers have been soldiers who came to power through coups: Idi Amin, Jean Bidel Bokassa, Etienne Gnassingbe Eyadema, Marcias Nguema, Mengistu Haile Mariam, Sani Abacha, Sassou Nguessou, Samuel Doe, Mamadou Tanja of Niger, Mobutu of Zaire, and Moussa Dadis Camara of Guinea. Besides, one coup always begets another, and that cannot be good for the stability and development of the country. There is nothing like a coup to end all coups.

If there is anything wrong with the political governance of the nation the solution to that problem should not be military intervention. The solution should lie ultimately with the sovereign people through popular revolt, provided the military does not interfere. Politicians resist removal by popular revolt only because they count on the military intervening on their side. If the military stays clear, as has happened in some East European countries, in Egypt and in Tunisia, no politician can possibly resist popular will. The problem with this proposed solution, it is conceded, is the uncertainty and susceptibility to manipulation of a mob. A mob is always fickle, uncontrollable, easily carried away, and susceptible to being hijacked by any glib-tongued, loquacious demagogue opportunistically bent on capturing power via the mob.

CORPORAL PUNISHMENT: SOLDIER BEATING CIVILIAN WITH A STICK

SOLDIERS ABUSING CIVILIAN

# Chapter 9

## Countries where there has been no Military Rule (Yet)

A number of African states have not experienced rule by the military. In some cases this is due to the fact that the soldiers respect the hallowed principle of an apolitical military and have shown no ambition for political power. In some other cases soldiers tried to seize power but failed in their attempt(s). Overall, in countries ruled by a national liberation movement that came to power (Angola, Mozambique, Namibia, South Africa, Zimbabwe) an army or insurgency overthrow of the government would seem infeasible for at least two reasons. Seemingly comrades in the same struggle and belonging to the same ideological school do not fight each other. Furthermore, the 'civilian' rulers and the country's soldiers were all freedom fighters. There is therefore no difference between both.

### Where no coup has been attempted

No attempt has ever been made by the military to seize power in the following ten countries:

Botswana
Djibouti
Eritrea
Malawi
Angola
Namibia
Mauritius
Sahrawi Arab Democratic Republic
South Africa (post-apartheid)
Republic of Southern Sudan
Swaziland

## Where a coup or an insurgency attempt failed

*Angola*

Angola's war of independence began in 1961 until 1975, when Portugal granted independence. Almost immediately, civil war broke out between the Zaire-based National Front (NF) of Holden Roberto, the US-backed National Union for the Total Independence of Angola (UNITA) of Jonas Savimbi, and the Soviet-backed Popular Movement for the Liberation of Angola (MPLA) of Agostinho Neto. On 27 May 1977 there was an attempted coup which "unrolled with incredible slowness, callous brutality and farcical incompetence over the next six days." (Birmingham 1978: 555) The coup leaders were Captain Nito Alves, Ernesto Gomes da Silva and José van Dunem. The coup was designed to kidnap President Agostinho Neto. It failed for the simple reason that the venue for the Central Committee meeting was changed fifteen minutes before the opening. Foolishly, Mobutu prematurely welcomed the announced overthrow of Neto. (Twenty years later, Mobutu would be paid back in his own coins when Angola intervened in the DRC in support of Kabila's insurgency against Mobutu). Angola's civil war which broke out in 1975 was officially ended in 1991 but fighting again broke out in 1992, when UNITA rejected the multiparty elections of that year and took once more to the bush. The country returned to normalcy following the killing of Savimbi and defeat of UNITA in 2005.

*Cameroun*

In 1955 the *Union des Populations du Cameroun* (UPC), Union of Cameroun Populations, launched a liberation struggle against French colonial rule in French Cameroun. France hurriedly granted independence to its French Cameroun territory on 1 January 1960 under French protective umbrella. The reins of formal power were handed to the pro-French politician, Ahmadou Ahidjo. The UPC characterized the independence as fake and Ahidjo as a French puppet. In fact, the independence ceremony in Yaoundé took place literally under a hail of bullets from UPC insurgents. The UPC vowed to continue the struggle until genuine independence was achieved under a nationalist government. The UPC insurgency continued until the end of 1970 when the remnants of the insurgents gave themselves up. The principal leaders of the insurgency, Ernest Ouandié and his lieutenants, were put through the motion of a trial by a military tribunal, sentenced to death and publicly executed in January 1971. The UPC insurgency was a particularly bloody affair in which the French army used overwhelming military force against the UPC. There was indiscriminate mass killing of civilians and the reported extermination of at least half a million people (Deltombe et al). This was probably the first but unacknowledged genocide committed in Africa. Throughout the next ten years rumours were rife of coups nipped in the bud. But in 1984 the real thing happened.

In November 1982, Biya was appointed President by his departing predecessor, Ahmadou Ahidjo. In early April 1984 Biya ordered a transfer of all soldiers of the *Garde Républicaine* (GR), presidential palace guards, who came from Ahidjo's predominantly Muslim north, and replaced them with those from his own tribal area. According to some accounts he had been alerted to a coup plot involving those soldiers. Dissident members of the GR promptly reacted to the order by rebelling against Biya. The leaders of the plot may have been forced to launch their coup attempt prematurely due to Biya's order to relocate the soldiers away from the capital, Yaoundé. The coup makers succeeded in taking the capital and for three days appeared in control. Biya had disappeared, hiding, as it later turned out, in a bunker underground below the *Palais Présidentiel*, the sort of tunnel hideout below state house seen in Abidjan when Gbagbo was captured and in Tripoli when Gadhafi was ousted. Biya's ministers had disappeared. Biya's government had practically collapsed. The general public appeared quite indifferent to the fate of Biya and his regime. But the coup makers vacillated, apparently undecided on whom to take over the reins of power and also unaware that the radio engineer had confined the reception of the coup broadcast to the capital. Troops loyal to Biya, mainly from his tribal constituency, rallied round. After several days of heavy and

117

savage fighting in Yaoundé, the coup was crushed. The government put the death toll at the very conservative and most improbable figure of 71. But other sources claim that as many as 1,000 people may have perished. More than 1,000 accused dissidents were arrested shortly afterward, and 35 of them were immediately sentenced to death and executed. There were unconfirmed reports of many other people extra-judicially executed and buried in mass graves around the town of Mbalmayo (Gaillard). The government declared a renewable six months state of emergency in Yaoundé and the surrounding region. Although Ahidjo was not overtly involved in the coup attempt, Biya and his government stated that he had masterminded it from exile and were not displeased to learn of Ahidjo's death in exile in Dakar in November 1989. The failure of the coup attempt was followed by Biya's assumption of dictatorial powers and marked the onset of totalitarian rule in that country and a despotism which many observers believe far worse than that of his predecessor.

*Gabon*

Between 17 and 18 February 1964 there was a coup by Gabonese military officers against President Léon M'ba. The coup resulted from M'ba's dissolution of the Gabonese legislature on 21 January 1964. There were a few casualties during the takeover. The 150 coup plotters arrested M'ba and a number of his government officials. In a radio broadcast, they asked the people of Gabon to remain calm and assured them that the country's pro-France foreign policy would remain unchanged. A provisional government was formed, and the coup's leaders named as the country's new president Jean-Hilaire Aubame, who was M'ba's main political opponent. M'ba was not hurt but was banished to Lamberéné, 250 kilometres (155 miles) from Libreville. There was no major uprising or reaction by the Gabonese people when they received word of the coup, which the military interpreted as a sign of approval.

The Gabonese army chief, Albert-Bernard Bongo, informed French President Charles de Gaulle of the coup. De Gaulle decided to reinstate the M'ba government, claiming he was doing so in terms of a 1960 Franco-Gabonese co-operation treaty which required France to intervene under such circumstances. On 19<sup>th</sup> February 1964 French troops forcibly landed in Libreville, toppled the provisional government, and re-instated M'ba as President of Gabon. M'ba quickly exacted revenge by imprisoning more than 150 of his opponents. Aubame was sentenced to 10 years of hard labour and 10 years of exile, a sentence that was later commuted. During this time, the ageing president became increasingly reclusive, opting to stay in his presidential palace under the protection of French troops. Within three years, M'ba was diagnosed with cancer. He died on 28 November 1967. Power was then handed over to Bongo who remained President of Gabon for 42 years. Bongo died in 2009. Power passed to his son with the blessing of the military.

*Kenya*

There was a Kenyan coup d'état attempt in 1982. It failed to overthrow President Daniel arap Moi's government. Its execution was at best amateuristic. A group of soldiers of the Kenyan Air Force, led by Private Hezekiah Ochuka, took over the radio station at midnight of 1 August 1982. They announced the overthrow of the government. The group tried to force some Air Force fighter pilots to bomb the State House. The pilots pretended to obey. They took off in their jets but once airborne they ignored the orders they had received and instead dropped their bombs at the forest around Mount Kenya. The revolt was quickly put down by loyalist forces consisting of the Army, the paramilitary wing of the police known as the General Service Unit (GSU), and the regular police. At least 150 civilians were killed in the drama.

Hezekiah Ochuka ruled Kenya for about six hours before escaping to Tanzania. He was subsequently extradited to Kenya where he was tried, convicted of treason and executed in 1987. Eleven other people were sentenced to death and executed, and over 900 were jailed. Jaramogi Oginga Odinga, former Vice President in Jomo Kenyatta's government, his son Raila Amolo Odinga, and the University were alleged to have been implicated in the attempted coup. This prompted the government to accuse external communist sources of having secretly funded the attempt. The failed coup attempt had other consequences. The entire Kenyan air force was disbanded. Moi called snap elections in 1983 which he won, thereby consolidating his hold on power.

*Morocco*

In 1971 there was an attempted coup that would have overthrown the Moroccan monarchy under King Hassan II. Three days after the failed coup, ten of the leading putschists were executed. In August 1972 there was another coup attempt. The attempt was orchestrated by General Mohamed Oufkir, a close adviser to the King. On August 16, three Northrop F-5 jets, acting on Oufkir's orders, intercepted Hassan's Boeing 727 as it returned from France. They then opened fire on the 727. However, the F-5's guns were only loaded with practice ammunition and not missiles, lessening their effectiveness.

One of the F-5 pilots also attempted to ram King Hassan's 727, but missed the jet. According to some reports, King Hassan (himself a pilot), grabbed the radio and told the rebel pilots, "Stop firing! The tyrant is dead!" Fooled, the rebel pilots broke off their attack. Hassan's plane landed safely at Rabat's airport, which was strafed by air force jets, killing eight and injuring 40. Kenitra Airport, where most of the rebellious air force officers were from, was surrounded and hundreds arrested. Oufkir was found dead of gunshot wounds later on August 16, ostensibly from suicide.

In early 2011 there were popular uprisings in Morocco. Some groups demanded the abolition of the monarchy while others demanded constitutional and other reforms. King Hassan II's son who succeeded him as King of Morocco at first resisted, then he vacillated, but he eventually had the good sense to accede to the demands of the people thereby saving his life and his throne. The uprising was ended.

## Mozambique

Mozambique became independent on 25 June 1975 with Samora Machel as President after a ten year war of independence against Portuguese colonial rule. In 1977 civil war broke out. The ruling party, Front for Liberation of Mozambique (FRELIMO), was from that year militarily challenged by the rebel Mozambique Resistance Movement (RENAMO) generously funded by Rhodesia and later apartheid South Africa. Over 900,000 died in fighting and from starvation. Five million civilians were displaced and many were made amputees by landmines, a legacy from the war that continues to plague Mozambique.

The Mozambican leader, President Samora Michel, was killed in 1986 when his plane was shot down over South African airspace by the apartheid regime. Fighting ended in 1992 with the signing of a peace agreement between FRELIMO and RENAMO. The country's first multi-party elections were held in October 1994. The presidential election was won by Joaquim Chissano.

## Senegal

In 1958 Senegal and the French Soudan united to form the Mali Federation. On 20 August 1960 the Federation broke up, each country regaining its previous status as a separate country. The French Soudan took the name Mali and Senegal retained its name. President Senghor and Prime Minister Mamadou Dia governed together under a parliamentary system.

In December 1962, the political rivalry between the two led to an attempted coup d'état by Dia. The coup was put down without bloodshed. Dia was arrested and imprisoned. Senegal adopted a new constitution that consolidated Senghor's power. After twenty years in power Senghor announced his retirement in January 1981. His handpicked successor, Abdou Diouf, took over and organized elections in 1982 which he won. He was re-elected in 1988 and again in 1993. In March 2000 he ran for a third term of office and lost against the opposition leader Abdoulaye Wade.

## Tanzania/Tanganyika

Tanganyika[78] achieved independence on 9 December 1961 under Nyerere. The country was independent but oddly the army, the Tanganyika Rifles, formerly the King's African Rifles, continued to be under foreign command, the command of British officers. The nascent State had very little national control over the army. Authority from its Ministry of Defence was minimal. Even as President, Nyerere had no regular interaction with Brigadier Douglas, the British commander of the army, and never discussed any high defence policy with him. There was thus a national army but without a defence or a foreign policy. The army simply ran its own affairs.

What was more, Tanganyikan officers were not privy to strategic military plans and the British army officers continued to discriminate against them. A debate in Parliament on this state of affairs in the army showed a House split between those who wanted a better equipped army and those who felt that the military posed a threat to democracy and for that reason had misgivings about having an army. One Member of Parliament argued that the country needed a military force but cautioned that government should not maintain the military so much so that it becomes the one that maintains the government.

When the OAU Liberation Committee was set up in Dar es Salaam, Nyerere initially thought of using the army as a tool for liberation of southern Africa but later discounted this possibility partly because the army was still under the command of British officers and partly because of the restive mood in the army barracks. Tanganyikan soldiers openly agitated for promotions, better conditions of service, for the removal of British officers, and for the Africanization of the army command. The British officers would have none of these.

---

[78] H Lupogo, 'Civil-Military Relations and Political Stability in Tanzania,' (2001) 10 (1) *African Security Review* 33; N Luanda, 'The Tanganyika Rifles and the Mutiny of January 1961', in Hutchful & Bathily (ed.), *The Military and Militarism in Africa*, CODESRIA, Dakar, 1998, p. 175.

The government got wind of this agitation. But while it was still studying these legitimate grievances the soldiers mutinied on 19 January 1964. The revolt began in Dar es Salaam and spread to other localities in the country. "For at least one week Nyerere was preoccupied with the mutiny. He dramatically disappeared for a couple of days while Kambona [Minister of Defence and of Foreign Affairs] tried to negotiate with the mutineers. Two days after he reappeared he sought assistance from the British. Sixty British marines bombarded the Calito barracks. Mutineers surrendered. Nyerere dissolved the army and rebuilt one from scratch while the Nigerian troops looked after his defence."[79]

Nyerere would later concede that the soldiers had genuine grievances, but said it was unacceptable that they should have resorted to a munity to air their grievances. Commentators have since argued that the mutiny was not a *coup* attempt because the soldiers never challenged the legitimacy of the political leadership, nor did they attempt to take over the government. For them the revolt was more in the nature of a strike over service conditions.

However, government's reaction to this incident suggests that it saw the revolt as a coup attempt rather than as a form of industrial action. Nyerere called in external intervention. He also decided to replace the colonially-inherited army with a people's army. He disband the army (tainted as it was by a rebellion whether in the form of a mutiny or an attempted coup), created a new and politically indoctrinated army from scratch, and integrated it into Tanzanian society. The way he went about it was straightforward.

Fresh recruits were enlisted from among members of the youth wing of the ruling party. Soldiers and other public officials were allowed to join the ruling party, the country at that time being a *de facto* one-party state. Membership of the ruling party became a prerequisite for enrolment in the army. The first recruits passed out

---

[79] I.G Shivji, *Pan-Africanism or Pragmatism? Lessons of Tanganyika-Zanzibar Union*, 2008, p. 54. The author cites W Smith, *We Must Run While They Walk: A Portrait of Africa's Julius Nyerere*, New York, Random House, 1971, pp. 149 bet seq.

in September 1964 as the Tanzania Peoples' Defence Force (TPDF). Political commissars were introduced into the army. Later, battalion-size units became party branches and every commander was party chairman in his command. Government inculcated into the soldiers that they were a people's force under civilian control, and with the mission of defending Tanzania, everything Tanzanian, the people and their political ideology.

The creation of a people's army did not however completely remove the ever-present temptation from those under arms to gun for political power. There has not been a *coup d'état* or a serious attempt at one in Tanzania. But that does not mean civil-military relations in that country have always been excellent. The nationalization of various properties in the country in 1969 under the policy of socialism and self-reliance triggered disgruntlement among many property owners who, according to some Tanzanian watchers, subsequently hatched a plot to overthrow the government. Four army officers were implicated in the plot which was quickly nipped in the bud and a *coup* avoided. The fact that the people's army was structured and organised in such a way that soldiers were in the political party and in government, and politicians were in the army, made it extremely difficult to get a substantial following for a *coup* plot. That is why even the later coup plot of 1982 also failed.

### Zanzibar[80]

The island of Zanzibar off the coast of Tanganyika achieved independence from Britain in December 1963 as a monarchy ruled by a Sultan. On 12 January 1964, barely a month after independence, the Sultanate and his Government was overthrown in a bloody insurrection. The immediate causes of the insurrection were the removal of all non-Zanzibari from the police force and the banning of political parties and societies considered undesirable or unlawful. The insurrection was conceived, planned and executed by the Youth

---

[80] I.G Shivji, *Pan-Africanism or Pragmatism? Lessons of Tanganyika-Zanzibar Union*, Mkuki na Nyato Publishers, Dar es Salam, 2008, pp. 41-64.

League of one of the banned political parties with the assistance of a resident daredevil Ugandan called John Okello who assumed the leadership of the insurrection. The group came to be known as the 'Committee of 14'.

The insurrectionists had some idea of overthrowing the government but did not know and had not planned as to what they would do with power after the fall of the government. Early on Sunday morning, a couple of hours after mid-night the insurrectionists attacked the police armoury, overrun it and captured arms which they then distributed among themselves. But they did not bother to capture the airport or the cable and wireless or cut off communication until much later. There were accidental and revenge killings as well as massacres in the surrounding and rural areas. Many Arabs were detained and later in the week boatloads of them were sent off to Muscat. By day dawn Okello announced in a fierce voice the overthrow of the Government. Within two days a Cabinet and a Revolutionary Council was formed with Abeid Karume as President. The People's Republic of Zanzibar was proclaimed. However, that Republic lasted a mere three months. On 22 April 1964 Tanganyika and Zanzibar united to form a single State known as United Republic of Tanzania.

### Zambia

The one party rule and the declining economy created disappointment among the people of Zambia. Several strikes hit the country in 1981. The government responded by arresting several union leaders, among them Frederick Chiluba. In 1986 and 1987 protests arose again in Lusaka and the Copperbelt. These were followed by riots over rising food prices in 1991, in which at least 30 people were killed. The same year the state owned radio claimed that Kaunda had been removed from office by the army. This was not true, and the coup attempt failed. President Kaunda called early presidential election in November 1991. He lost to Chiluba and he conceded defeat, statesman-like.

In 1993 the government owned newspaper "The Times of Zambia" reported a story about a secret plan by the United National Independent Party (UNIP) to take control of the Chiluba government by unconstitutional means. The plan was code-named the "Zero Operation Plan". The plan included industrial unrest, promotion of violence and organisations of mass protests. The UNIP did not deny the existence of such a plan, but underlined that it was not a part of their official policy, but the views of extremists within the party. The government responded by declaring a state of emergency and putting 26 people into detention. Of these seven, including Kenneth Kaunda's son Wezi Kaunda were charged with offences against the security of the state. The rest were released.

Prior to the 1996 elections, the UNIP formed an alliance with six other opposition parties. Kenneth Kaunda had earlier retired from politics, but after internal turbulence in the party, due to the "Zero Operation Plan" scandal, he returned, replacing his own successor Kebby Musokotwane. Chiluba's government then amended the constitution, banning people whose parents were not both Zambian citizens from becoming president. This was directly aimed at Kaunda, whose parents were both from Malawi. In protest the UNIP and its allies boycotted the elections, which were then easily won by Chiluba and the MMD.

In 1997 matters escalated. On 28 October a coup d'état took place, as a group of army commanders led by Captain 'Solo' took control over the national radio station, broadcasting a message stating that Chiluba was no longer president. The coup was brought to an end by regular forces, after Chiluba had again declared a state of emergency. One person was killed during the operation. After the failed coup the police arrested at least 84 people accused of involvement. Among these were Kenneth Kaunda and Dean Mungomba, leader of the opposition Zambia Democratic Congress political party. The arrests were condemned and criticised as illegal inside as well as outside Zambia, and accusations of torture were made as well. Kaunda was released in June the following year, but 44 of the soldiers who took part in the coup were sentenced to death in 2003

*Zimbabwe*

Ian Smith, Premier of the British colony of Southern Rhodesia, unilaterally declared on 11 November 1965 the independence of that country the name of which he had changed a year earlier to Rhodesia, *tout court*. The British Government termed the action illegal and demanded that Rhodesia broadens voting rights to provide for eventual rule by the majority Africans. The UDI sparked a 15-year national liberation struggle by Africans which ended with the independence of the country in 1980 under the name and style of Zimbabwe.

The Zimbabwean government foiled an alleged coup d'état attempt involving almost 400 soldiers and high-ranking members of the military that would have occurred on June 2 or June 15, 2007. The alleged leaders of the coup, all of whom were arrested and charged with treason, were retired army Captain Albert Matapo, Spokesman for the Zimbabwe National Army Ben Ncube, Major General Engelbert Rugeje, and Air Vice Marshall Elson Moyo.

According to the government the soldiers planned on forcibly removing President Robert Mugabe from office and asking Rural Housing Minister Emmerson Mnangagwa to form a government with the heads of the armed forces. The government first heard of the plot when a former army officer who opposed the coup contacted the police in Paris, France, giving them a map and a list of those involved. Mnangagwa and State Security Minister Didymus Mutasa both said they did not know about the plot, Mnangagwa calling it "stupid."

# Chapter 10

## Countries where there has been one coup (so far)

*Cape Verde*
The Cape Verde Islands achieved independence from Portugal in July 1975. The PAIGC was the only political organization in both Cape Verde and Guinea Bissau. In 1980 there was a coup d'état in Guinea Bissau. The coup ended the loose federation of Cape Verde and Guinea-Bissau. Plans for unification of the two former Portuguese territories were abandoned. The Cape Verde branch of the PAIGC was renamed PAIGV and a new constitution was adopted for the country. Another new constitution in 1991 introduced multiparty democracy. In the 1991 election, Antonio Mascarenhas Monteiro challenged and defeated Aristides Maria Pereira in power since 1975. Monteiro was re-elected without opposition in 1996. In 2001 Pedro Pires became the new President, served two 5-year terms and on 21 August 2011 Carlos Fonseca was elected President in a presidential runoff election.

*Côte d'Ivoire*
When Houphouët-Boigny died in 1995, Konan Bédié became President. In late 1999, a group of disgruntled officers staged a military coup and put General Robert Guéï in power. A presidential election was held in October 2000. Guéï's attempt to rig the election led to a public uprising in which many people lost their lives. Guéï was replaced by Laurent Gbagbo, the election's likely winner.

In September 2002 there was an armed uprising against Gbagbo. The rebel forces took control of the north of the country and threatened to move on Abidjan. France deployed troops and the rebel advance was halted. But the country was effectively divided into two, the north under rebel control and the south under government control. The government blamed the armed insurgency on an alleged coup attempt by former President Guéï and in which he was killed in the fighting that ensued between rebel and government forces.

In 2003, government and rebel leaders signed accords creating a 'government of national unity'. But the rebel forces refused to disarm. UN peacekeepers were deployed along a zone separating rebel-held north and government-held south. In 2006 there was an attempted coup against Laurent Gbagbo. In March 2007, a peace deal was signed between the government and the rebels (known as New Forces), whose leader Guillaume Soro, became Prime Minister. Presidential elections were held in 2010, pitting two main candidates, Gbagbo and Alassana Ouattarra. UN and other International election observers pronounced the elections as free and fair. The UN declared Ouattarra the winner. But Gbagbo refused to concede defeat and had himself sworn in as President. Ouattarra also had himself sworn in.

Ivory Coast had the undignified spectacle of finding itself with two rival presidents. Months of efforts by the UN, the AU and third states to get Gbagbo to give up his claim to the presidency failed. The stage was then set for a civil war which eventually broke out in early 2011. Forces supporting Gbagbo consisted of the Ivorian military and those supporting Ouattarra consisted of the rebel New Forces backed by French and UN intervention forces. The capture of Gbagbo who had taken refuge in the bunker under the Presidential House brought the civil war to an end.

*Egypt*

In 1952, Egypt set the example for the coups that would become a common occurrence all over Africa. In that year Brigadier Muhammad Neguib and Colonel Abdul Nasser deposed King Farouk in a military coup. Nasser became the new Egyptian leader. Upon Nasser's death, Anwar Sadat, another soldier took over. When Sadat was assassinated by his own soldiers, Mubarak became next President and remained in power until about mid-2011 when he was chased from power by a popular uprising that lasted months in what became known as the 'Arab Spring Democratic Awakening'. During the same period popular uprisings also sprung up in Tunisia and Libya and saw the end of the regimes in those countries.

*Equatorial Guinea*

In 1968, Spain granted Equatorial Guinea independence with Francisco Macias Nguema as its President. Nguema ruled with an iron fist. In December 1975 there was apparently an attempted coup against him. The coup failed. On Christmas day he had the alleged 150 coup plotters executed in a stadium, while a band played music. In 1979 Nguema's dictatorship was brought to an end following a military coup by Teodoro Obiang Nguema Mbasogo, his nephew, who then ushered in his own despotic rule.

In 2004 there was an alleged coup attempt against the government of Equatorial Guinea in order to replace President Teodoro Obiang Nguema Mbasogo with exiled opposition politician Severo Moto. The coup was to be carried out by mercenaries. It was organised by mainly British financiers. The allegation was that Equatorial Guinea's opposition leader, Severo Moto, was to be installed as the new president in return for preferential oil rights to corporations affiliated to those involved with the coup. The failed coup attempt received international media attention after the reported involvement of Sir Mark Thatcher, the son of the former British Prime Minister Margaret Thatcher, in funding the coup and mercenaries contracted to do the job. The mercenaries were intercepted when transiting through Zimbabwe, arrested, tried and jailed.

In March 2004 Zimbabwean authorities took 164 people into custody and seized a US-registered jetliner carrying military material. More than 60 men were charged as mercenaries with plotting to destabilise a sovereign government. In January 2005 Mark Thatcher pleaded guilty in a South African court to bankrolling an alleged coup plot in Equatorial Guinea in a plea bargaining deal.

## Gambia

Sir Jawara Daouda was President of The Gambia from independence in 1964 until his ousted from power in a coup by Captain Yaya Jammeh on 22 July 1994. Before this coup Sir Jawara had survived in 1981 a coup attempt by Kukoi Sanyang. Jawara owed his survival to Senegalese soldiers who helped to suppress the rebellion. In July 1994 Jawara was overthrown in a coup by Captain Jameh Yahya. Captain Yahya is still in power and amazingly has transformed Gambia from the backward State it was under Sir Jawara to the rapidly developing State it is today.

## Libya

Colonel Mu'ammar Gadhafi and Major Jalloud deposed King Idris in 1969 and seized power. In February 2011 a popular uprising broke out in Libya against Gadhafi. His savage repression of the revolt, using war planes to drop bombs on the unarmed protesters led to two major developments. First the peaceful uprising turned into an insurgency to topple the Gadhafi regime. Second the UN Security Council adopted a resolution by which NATO was empowered to take all necessary measures to ensure the protection of Libyan civilians against Gadhafi's armed onslaught. The insurgents quickly developed military capability backed by NATO bombing of Gadhafi military targets. After eight months of fighting, Gadhafi's forces were defeated in October 2011. Gadhafi and his son, a military commander, were captured and summarily executed by their captors on October 20th 2011.

## Seychelles

Seychelles gained independence from Britain in June 1976 under James Mancham. On 5 June 1977, with Mancham in London to attend the Commonwealth Conference, the supporters of Albert René, an opposition leader, staged a coup d'état and René assumed power. Mancham fled into exile. New elections were called in 1979 with René pitted against barrister Robert Frichot. René defeat Robert's party, allegedly through the use of military force. A one-party socialist state was established. It was alleged that after winning, René threatened to kill Robert and his family unless they left the country and so Frichot had to move to Perth, Australia.

On 25 November 1981, mercenaries led by "Mad" Mike Hoare attempted to take over the Seychelles, but were discovered at the airport. They briefly took over the airport control tower and hijacked an Air India flight to South Africa where they were arrested and charged. In August 1982, the Seychelles Army revolted because of alleged poor conditions in the military. They took over the radio station in what appeared to be an attempt to topple the government. René requested the intervention of Tanzania troops. The troops landed in Seychelles and put down the rebellion.

## Togo

Ex-Sergeants Bodjolle and Eyadema staged a coup in Togo in 1963, killing the country's President Sylvanius Olympio. An attempted counter coup by civil servants, an administrative coup, failed. Eyadema remained in power until his death in 2006. Power passed to his son by permission of the military.

## Tunisia

Zine El Abidine Ben Ali, President of Tunisia until March 2011, was previously a military officer. In 1987 he seized power from President Habib Bourguiba after a team of medical experts judged Bourguiba unfit to exercise the functions Head of State due to senility. The event is often described as a 'bloodless palace medical coup'. Prior to that moment Ben Ali was Bourguiba's minister. The day he seized power, 7 November, was until 2011 celebrated by Tunisia as national holiday.

In December 2006 and January 2007 clashes occurred in and around Tunis between a group of Islamist and the police in which 14 gunmen were killed. The incidents raised fears in the region that a loose network of militants was stepping up attempts to topple governments in the Maghreb. Thirty men were arrested and put on trial for attempting a coup. The men were said to belong to the Assad

Ibn Fourat Soldiers, an Islamist group with links to al Qaeda, according to the prosecution. The defendants were charged with attempting to overthrow the government of Ben Ali, disturbing public order and belonging to a terrorist group. While the case was still pending Ben Ali was ousted from power in March 2011 by a popular uprising. He fled the country together with his family.

# Chapter 11

## Countries where there has been more than one coup

*Algeria*

On 5 July 1962, Algeria gained independence from France after a long and bloody nationalist struggle. Ahmed Ben Bella became President of the new State. Three years later, in 1965, he was overthrown by a military coup that installed Colonel Houari Boumedienne as the new ruler. In January 1992, Government cancelled multiparty elections that the *Front Islamique du Salut* (FIS) political party was poised to win. That action gave rise to a protracted insurgency. In the same year Khaled Nezzar ousted Chadli Bendjedid from power.

*Benin*

On 28 October 1963, the Chief of Staff of the Dahomeyan Army Col. Christophe Soglo took control of the country ostensibly to prevent what appeared to be an incipient civil war. He dismissed the cabinet, dissolved the Assembly, suspended the constitution and banned any type of demonstrations. He forced President Hubert Maga to resign. On the same day he conferred the powers of Minister of State on Hubert Maga, Sourou-Migan Apithy, and Justin Ahomadégbé-Tomêtin, the triumvirate that had been running the country since independence from France in 1960. Soglo gave the following reasons for the overthrow of President Hubert Maga: "luxurious life style of the rulers, abusive increase in the number of ministerial posts, unsatisfied social demands, unkept promises, the rise of the cost of living, and antidemocratic measures that martyrized the people and reduced them to nothing." In December the same year Soglo handed power to Apithy, only to seize it back in December 1965. Soglo himself was overthrown in December 1968 by

Major Kouandete who then set up a military government under Lt Col. Alley.

In June 1969 power was again handed over to a civilian, Dr Emile Sinzou but in December the same year Kouandete dismissed Zinsou's government and set up a military triumvirate which ruled until May the following year when power was again handed to a civilian government led again by the triumvirate made of Hubert Maga, Apithy, and Ahomadegbe. The triumvirate managed to hold on to power for two years before being toppled by Major Mathieu Kerekou on 26 October 1972.

On 30 November 1975 Kerekou changed the name of the country by proclaiming the People's Republic of Benin. In January 1977 there was a coup attempt by a group of mercenaries led by the notorious Bob Denard. In 1988 there were two coup attempts that were foiled and in 1995 there were strong rumours of another foiled coup attempt. Kerekou stayed in power until 2001, except for a brief period from 1991-1996 when Nicephore Soglo, a civilian, served as President.

*Burkina Faso*

On August 5, 1960, Upper Volta attained full independence from France. The first president, Maurice Yaméogo, was the leader of the Voltaic Democratic Union (UDV). Soon after coming to power, Yaméogo banned all political parties other than the UDV. The government lasted until 1966 when after much unrest—mass demonstrations and strikes by students, labour unions, and civil servants—the military intervened.

The military coup deposed Yaméogo, suspended the constitution, dissolved the National Assembly, and placed Lt. Col. Sangoulé Lamizana at the head of a government made up of senior army officers. The army remained in power for four years, and on June 14, 1970, the Voltans ratified a new constitution that established a four-year transition period toward complete civilian rule. Lamizana remained in power throughout the 1970s as president of military or mixed civil-military governments. After conflict over the 1970 constitution, a new constitution was written and approved in 1977. Lamizana was re-elected in 1978. His government faced problems with the country's traditionally powerful trade unions.

On November 25, 1980, Col. Saye Zerbo overthrew President Lamizana in a bloodless coup and established the Military Committee of Recovery for National Progress as the supreme governmental authority, thus abrogating the 1977 constitution. It was not long before he also encountered resistance from trade unions and was overthrown two years later, on November 7, 1982, by Maj. Dr. Jean-Baptiste Ouédraogo and the *Conseil du Salut Populaire*, (CSP), Council of Popular Salvation. The CSP continued to ban political parties and organizations, yet promised a transition to civilian rule and a new constitution.

Factional infighting developed between moderates in the CSP and the radicals, led by Capt. Thomas Sankara, who was appointed Prime Minister in January 1983. The internal political struggle and Sankara's leftist rhetoric led to his arrest and subsequent efforts to bring about his release, directed by Capt. Blaise Compaoré. This release effort resulted in yet another military coup d'état on August 4, 1983. After the coup, Sankara formed the *Conseil National pour la Révolution* (CNR), National Council for the Revolution, with himself as President. Sankara also established the *Comités pour la Défense de la Révolution* (CDR), Committees for the Defence of the Revolution (CDR) to "mobilize the masses" and implement the CNR's revolutionary programs. The CNR, whose exact membership remained secret until the end, contained two small intellectual Marxist-Leninist groups. Four leftist military officers dominated the regime: Captain Sankara, Captain Compaore, Captain Henri Zongo, and Major Jean-Baptiste Lingani.

On August 4, 1984 Sankara changed the name of the country from Upper Volta to Burkina Faso, which means *"pays des hommes intègres"* ("land of people of integrity"). On 15 October 1987 Sankara was assassinated in a coup that brought Blaise Campaoré to power and he has remained in power since then. On Christmas eve of 1989 Campaoré had arrested thirty civilians and soldiers on charges of fomenting a coup with the collaboration of Burkinabé external opposition. In mid-2011 there was a military revolt in Ouagadougou, the capital, in what appeared to be an attempt to oust Campaore from power. Campaore disappeared and took refuge in his tribal region. He re-emerged in the capital a few days later and re-asserted his power.

## Burundi

On achieving independence from Belgium Burundi established a constitutional monarchy. In the 1961 elections leading up to independence, Louis Rwagasore, the son of the Tutsi Mwami and a popular politician and anti-colonial activist, was elected as Prime Minister. However, he was soon assassinated. The monarchy, with the aid of the military, therefore assumed control of the country, and allowed no further elections until 1965. In 1966 Captain Micombero seized power and deposed King Ntare V. In 1987 Buyoya deposed Jean-Baptiste Bagaza and in October 1993 Col Bagaza, Bikomagu and Ningaba assassinated the democratically elected President of Burundi, Melchior Ndandaye. On 25 July 1996, Major Pierre Buyoya seized power a second time by ousting the civilian government of President Sylvestre Ntibantunganya. For years Burundi relapsed into communal self-destruction but was later able to pick itself up.

## Central African Republic

The first President of the country, Barthelemy Boganda, died in a suspicious plane accident. At once there ensued for a few years a struggle for power between his former aids. David Dacko eventually became President. But in 1966 he was ousted in a military coup by his own cousin, Col. Jean Bedel Bokassa who in 1972 declared himself President for life. A few years later, in 1976, Bokassa decreed the country an 'Empire' and crowned himself its 'Emperor'.

The French, who had all along supported Bokassa later turned against him, removed him from power and brought Daco back to power. That was in 1979. The French-led coup was codenamed *Opération Barracuda*. But Dacko barely lasted two years. In 1981 André

Kolimba seized power from him. Following presidential elections, power passed to civilians under Ange-Félix Patassé. In 2003 Patassé was overthrown in a military coup led by François Bozizé. In 2005 two armed rebellions broke out in the north of the country but were crushed a year by troops from France.

## Chad

In 1966, a Muslim insurgency by the *Front pour la Libération Nationale* (FROLINAT), Front for National Liberation, was launched in the north of the country. Chad's army proved incapable of dealing with it. François Tombalbayé, the Chadian President became increasingly distrustful of the army. France advised him to have a mixed government by sharing power with the military leadership. Heeding the French advice he reserved a place in his party for the army commander. Rumours of a military coup d'état were rife. In 1971 Gen Jacques Doumro was arrested; in 1973 Gen Félix Malloum was arrested, and in 1975 Gen Negue Djogo was arrested.

Tombalbaye undertook a general purge of the army, gendarmerie and police. The military had had enough and decided to hit back. On April 13th 1975 a military coup was staged. It was a very bloody affair which ended with the death of the President. The jailed officers were freed and Malloum made head of the usurper government. Malloum survived barely four years and was removed by another coup. He fled the country. His successor, Goukouni Ouéddei was replaced in 1982 by Hisène Habré, himself replaced in 1990 by Idriss Deby Itno who has been in power ever since, surviving several coup attempts thanks to French military support and protection.

## Comoros

On 6 July 1975, the Comorian Parliament passed a unilateral resolution declaring independence from France. Ahmed Abdallah proclaimed the independence of the Comorian State and became its first president. On 3 August 1975, French mercenary Bob Dénard ousted Ahmed Abdallah from office in an armed coup. He did so with clandestine support from French Minister Jacques Foccart and the French government. Abdallah was replaced with Said Mohammed Jaffar. Months later, in January 1976, Jaffar was ousted in favour of his Minister of Defence Ali Soilih.

Incredibly, on 13 May 1978, Bob Dénard returned to the Conmoros, overthrew President Soilih and re-instated Abdallah with the support of the French Government and the government of apartheid South African. During Soilih's brief rule, he faced seven additional coup attempts until he was finally forced from office and killed.

Abdallah continued as president until 1989 when, fearing a probable coup d'état, he signed a decree ordering the Presidential Guard, incredibly led by Bob Dénard, to disarm the armed forces. Shortly after the signing of the decree, Abdallah was allegedly shot dead in his office by a disgruntled military officer. Although Dénard was also injured, it is suspected that Abdallah's killer was a soldier under Dénard's command. A few days later, Bob Dénard was evacuated to South Africa by French paratroopers. Soilih's older half-brother, Said Mohamed Djohar, then became President and served until September 1995 when Bob Dénard returned yet again and attempted another coup. This time France intervened with paratroopers and forced Dénard to surrender. The French removed Djohar to Réunion, and the Paris-backed Mohamed Taki Abdulkarim became President. Abdulkarim led the country for two years, from 1996 to November 1998 when he died. He was succeeded by an interim President, Tadjidine Ben Said Massounde.

In April 1999, Colonel Azali Assoumani, Army Chief of Staff, seized power in a bloodless coup, overthrowing the interim President Massounde. Assoumani gave as justification for his coup weak leadership in the face of the Anjouan and Moheli crises. This was the Comoros' 18th coup d'état since independence in 1975. But Assoumani failed to consolidate power and to re-establish control over the two rebel islands. The African Union imposed sanctions on Anjouan to help broker negotiations and effect reconciliation. The official name of the country was changed to the Union of the

Comoros and a new system of political autonomy for each island, plus a union government for the three islands.

Assoumani stepped down in 2002 to run in the democratic election for the President of the Comoros, which he won. As a military ruler who had originally come to power by force and was not always democratic while in office, Assoumani was under international pressure and successfully led the Comoros through constitutional changes that enabled new elections. A law was passed in early 2005 that defined the responsibilities of each governmental body. The elections in 2006 were won by Ahmed Abdallah Mohamed Sambi. Colonel Mohammed Bacar, a French-trained former gendarme officer, had seized power as President in Anjouan in 2001. In June 2007 he staged a vote to confirm his leadership. The vote was rejected as illegal by the Comoros federal government and the African Union. On March 25, 2008 hundreds of soldiers from the African Union and Comoros seized the rebel-held Anjouan. This was generally welcomed by the population. Since independence from France, the Comoros has experienced more than 20 coups or attempted coups.

*Republic of the Congo*

In 1963 Alphonse Massemba-Débat was replaced by Father Fulbert Youlou. The Rev Father was overthrown in 1968 by Captain Marien Ngouabi. In 1977 Joachim Yhombi-Opango carried out a coup in which Ngouabi was killed. But barely two years later, in 1979, Denis Sassou-Nguessou seized power from Yhombi-Opango in another coup. In 1992, following presidential elections which were won by Pascal Lissouba, leader of the *Union Panafricaine pour la Démocratie Sociale* (UPADS), power was handed back to civilians. But just one year later, in 1993, armed civil rebellion broke out and continued for months. Lissouba's government forces fought against three main armed militia groups, his own 'Zulu' militia, Bernard Kolelas' 'Ninja' militia, and Sassou-Nguessou's 'Cobra' militia.

In October 1997, after four years of civil war, Sassou-Nguessou's 'Cobras', aided by Angolan forces, defeated the combined 'Zulu' and

'Ninja' militias. Lissouba was toppled and Sassou-Nguessou seized power a second time. He had himself sworn in as President, thus becoming the 'old new' ruler of Congo. Lissouba fled the country into exile as he had done in the late seventies when his life sentence for involvement in the death of Ngouabi was commuted to banishment. He went to Burkina Faso and then eventually to the UK. In 1999 Sassou-Nguessou had Lissouba tried in absentia for high treason, for plotting to kill Sassou-Nguessou, for embezzlement of public funds, and, significantly, for sale of oil to an American firm at a low price. He was convicted and got thirty years. Sassou-Nguessou is still in power.

### Democratic Republic of the Congo

In 1960, Mobutu staged a coup against Lumumba and in 1965 against Kasavubu. Mobutu then appointed himself President and held on to power, surviving many coup and insurgency attempts, until 1997 when he was ousted by an armed insurgency led by Laurent Kabila. He escaped into exile in Togo where shortly afterwards he died of prostate cancer. Laurent Kabila was killed in 2001 by one of his body guards. His son Joseph Kabila became the next president of the country and has had to crush at least two coup attempts in 2004.

### Ethiopia

In September 1928, in Addis Ababa, a group of palace reactionaries made a final bid to rid the Empress Zewditu of Tafari. The group included some of Zewditu's courtiers. The attempted *coup d'état* was tragic in its origins and comic in its end. When confronted by Tafari and a company of troops, the ringleaders of the coup took refuge on the palace grounds in Menilek's mausoleum. Tafari and his men surrounded them only to be surrounded themselves by the personal guard of Zewditu. More of Tafari's khaki clad soldiers arrived and surrounded Zewditu's guard. Tafari's soldiers were equipped with newly imported rifles, machine guns, small cannon, and an obsolete but menacing tank. The tank, a Fiat 3000, had been a gift to Empress Zewditu from the Duke of Abruzzi of Italy during a visit some years earlier. In the end, the superiority of arms of the forces supporting Tafari decided the outcome in his favour.

In 1960 there was an abortive revolution. In 1974 Gen Aman Andom at the head of the Dergue staged a coup, deposed Emperor Haile Selassie, and seized power. Later, Andom was overthrown by Gen Mengistu Haile Mariam who in turn was overthrown in 1991 by Gen Tesfaye Gebre Kidan. In the same year Birhanu Bayeh seized power from Gebre Kidan. Meneles would later become the new strong man of the country.

*Ghana*

On 24 February 1966, Generals Harlley, Kotoka, Afrifa, Ocran and Ankrah overthrew Kwame Nkrumah in a military coup and seized power. At the time of his overthrow Nkrumah was abroad trying to broker peace in the then troubled Vietnam. The coup was particularly bloody because the rebel soldiers encountered stiff and sustained resistance from the presidential guards. Afrifa justified the coup *ex post facto* in these terms:

> "A coup in itself is not a good thing; but it is one of the most effective methods of restoring the constitutional rights of the people when they have been deprived of the constitutional means for changing a corrupt and tyrannical government. ... The aim of the unconstitutional military action we took is to regain ... freedom and to create the conditions and atmosphere in which true democracy can thrive." (Afrifa 1966:85)

It is believed by many political analysts that the United States Central Intelligence Agency participated in the coup against Nkrumah, but others claim that the evidence pointing to CIA involvement is anecdotal. General Kotoka became President following the putsch but was killed in April 1967 in an attempted coup. He was replaced by General Ankrah who quickly started lining his pockets. He was forced to resign following a big corruption scandal in which he was heavily involved.

There was a brief spell of civilian rule under Koffi Busia, from 1970-1972. In 1972, General Acheampong overthrew the Busia government and declared himself President. He held on to power for six years. He was overthrown in July 1978 by General Akuffo who, a year later, returned power to a civilian government led by Hilla Limann. But just a few months later, in May 1979, there was an attempted coup by Flight-Lieutenant Jerry Rawlings. Following the failure of the coup Rawlings was arrested, court-martialled, and detained pending sentencing.

But a few weeks later, in June, a group of middle level soldiers stormed the prison, released Rawlings, and made him the new military chief. The surviving generals who had overthrown Nkrumah were arrested, tied to the stake and publicly executed. Six months later, on 31$^{st}$ December, Rawlings put an end to Limann's limping and ineffectual government. The overthrow of Limann did not surprise anyone. Rawlings became the new Ghanaian Head of State and remained in power for twenty years. When Rawlings took over the military government remained in charge until 1992 when Rawlings shed his military uniform, ran for president as a civilian, won the election, and remained in power until 2000 when he was constitutionally barred from running for a third term. John Kuffour won the election of that year and in January 2001 took over the reins of power in Ghana. He served two terms, having again beaten John Atta Mills in 2004. In 2009 Mills won the presidential elect by the slimmest of margins (40, 000 votes) and took over office as president. That peaceful change of government marked the second time power had been transferred from one legitimately elected leader to another, securing Ghana's status as a stable democracy in Africa.

*Guinea*

Ahmed Sékou Touré became President upon Guinea's independence in 1958. In 1970 an attempt by white mercenaries to overthrow the government was defeated. Sekou Touré remained

President of Guinea until 26 March 1984, when he died unexpectedly. In the same year the successor civilian government was toppled by coup d'état led by Lansana Conté who then declared himself President. By despotic means, Conté clung to power until his death in 2008.

Shortly after Conté's death, Moussa Dadis Camara, on 23 December 2008, seized control of Guinea as the head of a military junta. On 28 September 2009, the junta ordered its soldiers to attack people who had gathered to protest any attempt by Camara to become President. The soldiers reportedly went on a rampage of rape, mutilation, and murder. On 3 December 2009, Camara's *Aide de Camp* shot him in the head during a dispute about the rampage of September 2009. Camara survived the shooting but was flown to Morocco for medical treatment. Vice-President and defence minister, Sékouba Konaté then took over as the new ruler of the country in Camara's absence. On January 12, 2010 Camara was flown from Morocco to Ouagadougou in Burkina Faso where, on January 13 and 14, the Burkinabé President, Blaise Campaoré, held a meeting with Camara and Konaté that produced a formal statement of twelve principles promising a return of Guinea to civilian rule within six months. It was agreed that the military would not contest the forthcoming elections, and that Camara would continue his convalescence outside Guinea. On 21 January 2010 the military junta appointed Jean-Marie Doré as Prime Minister of a six-month transition government, leading up to elections. The six months expired with no elections. Election was put off to 2011.

*Guinea-Bissau*

In the early 1960s, the African Party for the Independence of Guinea and Cape Verde (PAIGC), under the leadership of Amilcar Cabral, launched an anti-colonial guerrilla war against the Portuguese authorities. But the noted Pan-African intellectual and founder of the PAIGC was assassinated in Conakry by the Portuguese in 1973. His half-brother, Luis Cabral became leader of the Guinea-Bissau branch of the party. The overall party leadership for both Guinea-Bissau and

Cape Verde fell to Aristides Pereira. Aristides Pereira would later become the President of Cape Verde. Following a military coup in April 1974 at Lisbon, the new left-wing revolutionary government of Portugal granted independence to Guinea-Bissau, effective on September 10 that same year.

The PAIGC had unilaterally proclaimed the country's independence one year before in the village of Madina do Boé, and this event had been recognized by many socialist and non-aligned member states of the United Nations. Luís Cabral became President of Guinea-Bissau. But some suspicion and instability was present in the party since Amilcar Cabral's death and independence. Some sections of the party accused Luís Cabral and the other members with Cape Verdean origins of dominating the party. This was the reason given by Cabral's Prime Minister and former armed forces commander Joao Bernado Vieira when he carried out his coup d'état against Luis Cabral on 14 November 1980. Luís Cabral was then arrested and detained for 13 months. After the military coup in 1980, he was sent into exile, first in Cuba, which offered to receive him, then (in 1984), in Portugal, where the Portuguese Government received him and provided for his upkeep and that of his family, until his death in May 2009. On 22 October 1999, Vieira himself was toppled by General Asumane Mané. Then there followed a brief spell of civilian rule under President Kumba Yala.

But on 12 September 2003, a group of Guinea Bissau soldiers overthrew Yala and arrested him together with his Prime Minister, Mario Pires. The army advised the population to remain calm and avoid acts of vandalism. It admitted it carried out an "unconstitutional coup d'état" but argued that the coup was due to the "incapacity of the Yala regime to resolve the essential problems facing the people of the country."

In November 2008 there was an attempted coup seemingly led by the Navy Chief, Rear Admiral José Americo Bubo Na Tchuto, but which was foiled. Mutinous soldiers engaged in a three hour gun battle in the home of President Vieira who managed to escape unscathed. Rear Admiral Tchuto, apparently the coup mastermind, escaped to The Gambia. In 2009 there was yet another coup. Then on 1 April 2010 there was apparently a coup attempt. On that day civil unrest intensified in the country following what appeared to be an attempted coup by General Antonio Indjai. The General however stated that kidnapping and detention of the Prime Minister, Mr. Gomes Junior, and Army Chief, Gen Jose Zamora Induta, was as a result of an internal military problem, and not a coup. He gave the public assurance that military institutions remain, and will remain, submissive to political power. Hundreds of people took to the streets to demand the release of Prime Minister Gomes Junior. President Malam Bacai Sanha played down this latest incident, saying the situation was under control. In December 2011 an attempted military coup was foiled. But another coup attempt in April 2012 succeeded but this success was short-lived as there was another coup a month later. It is not clear what it is that fuels the periodic coups in this small poor country but some political watches put it on unrelenting power struggle and that country as a drug traffic transit hub.

## Lesotho

Chief Leabua Jonathan's rule as Prime Minister of Lesotho was abruptly ended by a military coup on 20 January 1986. An edict was issued vesting legislative and executive authority in the King, Moshoeshoe II. A Military Council was created with Major General Metsing Lekhanya as its Chairman and also Chairman of the Council of Ministers. There was thus ushered in Lesotho a curious military-cum-monarchical system of governance and the country was quickly dubbed a 'military Kingdom'. Not surprisingly, a struggle soon emerged within the Military Council and within the Council of Ministers between two factions, the pro-monarchy and the pro-military. This bitter struggle led to the coup of 19 February 1990.

## Liberia

On April 12, 1980, Samuel Kanyon Doe, a master sergeant in the Liberian army, led a very bloody *coup d'état* that toppled the government of President Tolbert. Tolbert and 26 of his supporters were killed and ten days later 13 of Tolbert's ministers were publicly executed at the beach. Doe established a military regime called the People's Redemption Council (PRC).

Doe survived seven coup attempts between 1981 and 1985. In August 1981 he had Thomas Weh Syen and four other PRC members arrested and executed for allegedly conspiring against him. In November 1985 Thomas Quiwonkpa, Doe's former second-in-command, with an estimated 500 to 600 people, failed in an attempt to seize power; all were killed. In the late 1980s, Charles Taylor assembled rebels into a militia. In 1989 he invaded Liberia from the northeast, and by 1990 a full-blown civil war was taking place. Taylor had served in Doe's government from 1980 until 1983 when he was sacked on accusation of embezzling government funds. He fled Liberia, was arrested in 1984 in Massachusetts on a Liberian warrant for extradition, and jailed in Massachusetts; escaped from jail in 1985.

By the middle of 1990, Taylor controlled much of the country, and by June laid siege on Monrovia. In July, Yormie Johnson split off from Taylor's militia and created his own. But both continued the siege on Monrovia. Bloodshed was all over. In August 1990, ECOWAS created a military intervention force called ECOMOG of 4,000 troops, to restore order. President Doe and Yormie Johnson agreed to this intervention, Taylor did not. On 9 September, President Doe paid a visit to the barely established headquarters of ECOMOG in the Free Port of Monrovia. While at the ECOMOG headquarters he was captured by Johnson's militia. The militia force took him to its base where he was tortured in a most barbaric manner and killed. In November 1990, ECOWAS agreed with key Liberian stakeholders (without Charles Taylor), on an Interim Government (IGNU) under President Dr. Amos Sawyer. Sawyer established his authority over most of Monrovia, with the help of a paramilitary police force. But the rest of the country remained in the hands of various warring factions.

In 1993, ECOWAS brokered a peace agreement in Cotonou, Benin. On 22 September 1993, the UN established an observer mission UNOMIL to support ECOMOG in implementing the

Cotonou Agreement. In March 1994, the interim government of Sawyer was succeeded by a Council of State collective presidency of six members headed by David D. Kpormakpor. In May 1994, renewed armed hostilities broke out and held on. Factional leaders agreed in September 1994 to the Akosombo peace agreement in Ghana. But it was of little consequence. In October 1994, the UN reduced its number of UNOMIL observers to about 90 because of the lack of will of combatants to honour peace agreements. Although factions and parties signed the Accra agreement in December 1994, fighting continued. In August 1995, factions including Charles Taylor signed an agreement largely brokered by Jerry Rawlings, the Ghanaian President. In September 1995, Kpormakpor's Council of State was succeeded by one under civilian Wilton Sankawulo. Sankawulo's Council of State included the three warlords Charles Taylor, Alhaji Kromah and George Boley. There was a brief lull in fighting. But in April 1996, fighting again resumed leading to the collapse of the peace accord. In August 1996, a new ceasefire was reached in Abuja, Nigeria. On 3 September 1996, Ruth Perry succeeded Sankawulo as chairwoman of the Council of State, with the same three warlords still present in it.

Charles Taylor won the 1997 presidential elections with 75 per cent of the vote. But bloodshed in Liberia did not end. Violence kept flaring up. During his entire reign, Taylor had to fight insurgencies against his government. Taylor was suspected of providing assistance in the form of weapons in exchange for diamonds, to rebel forces in neighbouring Sierra Leone.

In 1999, some militia forces emerged in northern Liberia and in April 2000 they started fighting in the north of the country. By the first quarter of 2001 they were posing a major threat to the Taylor government. Liberia was now engaged in a complex three-way conflict with Sierra Leone and the Republic of Guinea. Meanwhile, the United Nations Security Council in March, 2001 adopted Resolution 1343 in which it concluded that Liberia and Charles Taylor played roles in the civil war in Sierra Leone. The Council therefore banned arms sale to and diamond sales from Liberia. It also imposed a travel ban on members of the Liberian government. By the beginning of 2002, Sierra Leone and Guinea were supporting the anti-Taylor rebels, while Taylor was supporting opposition factions in both countries. By supporting Sierra Leonean rebels, Taylor also drew the enmity of the British and Americans and this eventually led to his ouster from power, his arrest and his indictment in and conviction by the International Criminal Court for crimes against humanity.

*Madagascar*

The political situation in Madagascar has always been marked by struggle for control. After Madagascar gained independence from France in 1960, assassinations, military coups and disputed elections featured prominently. Didier Ratsiraka took power in a military coup in 1975 and ruled until 2001, with a short break when he was ousted in the early 1990s. When Ratsiraka and Marc Ravalomanana both claimed victory after presidential elections in December 2001, Ratsiraka's supporters tried to blockade the capital, Antananarivo, which was pro-Ravalomanana. After eight months of sporadic violence with considerable economic disruption, a recount in April 2002 led the High Constitutional Court to pronounce Ravalomanana president, but it was not until July that Ratsiraka fled to France and Ravalomanana gained control of the country.

Protests over worsening standards of living preceded the presidential election announced for December 2006. Ravalomanana was one of several presidential candidates. One other candidate was a retired army general, Andrianafidisoa, also known as Fidy. He was disqualified from the presidential race for failing to pay the required deposit of 25 million Madagascar ariary (about US$11,400). An alleged coup d'état attempt occurred on 18 November 2006 when Fidy declared military rule. Fidy had previously supported the incumbent President Marc Ravalomanana in his successful claim to the presidency in the wake of the disputed 2001 presidential election. He probably expected Ravalomanana to support his presidential bid. Violence erupted when Fidy declared military rule.

President Ravalomanana was returning from France during the incident and his plane was diverted from Antananarivo to Mahajanga instead. The following day the government issued a wanted poster for Fidy and dozens of soldiers for an attack on state security. In a radio interview on 20 November Fidy, denied that there had been a coup attempt, but acknowledged that he had called for Ravalomanana's resignation because he considered the government to be unconstitutional. The presidential election billed for 3 December went ahead as planned. Ravolamanana was the controversial winner. There was a $50,000 bounty on Fidy and a week later he was arrested and put on trial. His defence was that he had not attempted a coup, but had instead attempted to alert Ravalomanana to the situation of the armed forces. He was sentenced to four years in prison on 2 February 2007. Ravolamanana's stay in power was to last only a couple of years.

On 26 January 2009 there began a power tussle between Marc Ravalomanana and Andry Rajoelina, former mayor of the capital, Antananarivo. More than 170 people were killed in the power struggle. Rajoelina mobilized his supporters to take to the streets of Antananarivo to demand Ravalomanana's ousting on the grounds of his alleged "autocratic" style of government. Two months later, in March 2009, the 34-year old former disc jockey, Rajoelina, said he had a mandate to lead a transitional government and that President Ravalomanana no longer had the mandate to run the country. "I have the mandate of more than 60 political parties in Madagascar to lead this transition, so it isn't a coup at all. We elected him (Mr. Marc Ravalomanana) to respect the law and the constitution. He cannot do whatever he likes with the country. So for us this President no longer has the right, nor the power any longer to run the country," said Mr. Rajoelina who then ordered the military to storm the presidential palace and offices.

Newly installed chief of army staff, Colonel Ndriarijaona threw his weight and that of the army wholly behind the opposition. The army seized the presidential palace with the intention to hasten the president's departure. Several soldiers loyal to Mr. Rajoelina stormed one of the Madagascar presidential palaces smashing down the palace gate with an armoured tank while letting off explosives and gunshots, before taking over the palace. Another faction of the pro-opposition army took over the central bank about the same time.

Ravalomanana took refuge in another palace in the city centre, protected by hundreds of his supporters. He told his guards, 'I will die with you if I have to,' and then went on to ask for military support from the UN and southern African states. But after losing the support of the military, the support of his ministers who deserted him one by one and under intense pressure from Rajoelina, President Ravalomanana resigned on 17 March 2009. He left a signed note in which he assigned his powers to a military council loyal to himself and headed by Vice-Admiral Hyppolite Ramaroson. The military called the move by Ravalomanana a "ploy" and supported Rajoelina as leader, in effect conferring power on him. Rajoelina had already declared himself the new leader a month earlier and had since assumed the role of acting President. He appointed Monja Roindefo as Prime Minister. He announced that elections would be held in two years and that the constitution would be amended.

The European Union and other international organisations refused to recognize the new government saying it had assumed power by force. The African Union (AU) suspended Madagascar's membership on 20 March 2009. The AU along with the Southern Africa Development Community (SADC) criticized the forced resignation of Ravalomanana. United Nations Secretary-General Ban Ki-moon's spokesperson said he was "gravely concerned about the evolving developments in Madagascar". All these disapproving statements apart, it was business as usual. As of the end of 2011 Mr. Rajoelina was still in power.

*Mali*

President Modibo Keita who in 1960 had led French Soudan to independence as the Sudanese Republic and then as the Republic of Mali was ousted from power in a military coup led by Col Moussa Traoré in 1968. In 1991 there was a popular uprising against

President Moussa Traoré. Colonel Amadou Toumani Touré intervened militarily and ousted Traoré from power. He assumed power for six months and immediately proceeded to draft a new constitution for the country. He put in place multi-party politics. He organized free and fair municipal, parliamentary and presidential elections in April 1992. He did not run in any of those elections. Alpha Oumar Konaré won the presidential poll and Toumani went back to the military barracks. Konaré served two consecutive terms and was prevented to stand again because of the two-term limit. Toumani Touré shed his military uniform, ran for elections in 2002 and won. He became Malian President. Konaré got the key job of Chairman of the African Union Commission where he served two terms.

On 21 March 2012, just a month before presidential elections were due in the country, President Toumani Touré was ousted from power by an apparently bloodless coup. The coup-makers, led by Captain Amadou Sanogo, justified their action on what they said was Toumani Touré's failure to deal effectively with the Tuareg rebellion in the north of the country and failure to provide the military with adequate weapons to defeat the insurgency. The country's defence minister was on an inspection tour of military barracks north of the capital, Bamako, when the coup-makers struck. Soldiers fired in the air during the inspection, prompting an immediate movement of armoured vehicles to strengthen security around the presidential palace.

There was heavy gunfire in the capital throughout the day and night as the coup-makers traded gunfire with soldiers loyal to the government. The putschists arrested a number of ministers including the foreign minister. They seized radio and television, identified themselves as the 'Committee for the Re-establishment of Democracy and the Restoration of the State', and imposed a national curfew. Their spokesman, Lt Amadou Konare, said they had ended the 'incompetent regime' of President Amadou Toumani Touré. He condemned the 'inability' of the government to 'fight terrorism', and said the soldiers would hand over to a democratically elected government. The United States and France urged the soldiers and government to resolve their dispute through peaceful means.

ECOWAS unrealistically called for the re-instatement of the ousted President, the restoration of constitutional rule, and threatened economic sanctions. Days afterwards the political situation in Mali worsened when the Tuaregs captured the northern two-thirds of the country and proclaimed an independent Azawad state with capital in Gao. The EU and the AU promptly declared they would not recognise the declared state and called for respect for the territorial integrity of Mali. Faced with this secessionist bid the new Mali military rulers bowed to ECOWAS pressures to hand over power to civilian rule. On Friday 13 April 2012 the Speaker of the Mali National Assembly, Mr. Dioncounda Traore, 70, was appointed as Mali's interim President and sworn-in by the President of the Mali Supreme Court. He had two immediate tasks: end the Tuareg secessionist bid, and organise free and fair elections within the shortest possible time.

The Mali coup-makers were in office for just 23 days. But they remained very much in the wings. It was not long before their supporters and those of the interim President clashed in the streets. In the last week of May 2012 there was a violent confrontation between the two sides around State House during which the interim President was said to have been assaulted, sustained injuries and had to be flown to France for treatment. The pro-military protesters claimed that the interim President's stay in office was over and that the leader of the March 2012 coup should assume the interim presidency as transitional leader. Meanwhile the Tuareg challenge remained unresolved. Apart from a verbal re-affirmation of Mali's territorial integrity, the transitional leaders seemed unable to confront the secessionist bid in the north; and, judging from the violent confrontation around the presidential palace it seemed they were also unable to guarantee even their own safety.

*Mauritania*

After independence in November 1960, President Moktar Ould Daddah, originally installed by the French, formalized Mauritania into a one-party state in 1964 with a new constitution, which set up an authoritarian presidential regime. He was ousted in a bloodless coup on 10 July 1978, after bringing the country to near-collapse through a disastrous war to annex the southern part of Western Sahara, in an attempt to create a "Greater Mauritania".

Col. Mustafa Ould Salek's *junta* proved incapable of either establishing a strong base of power or extracting the country from its destabilizing conflict with the Sahrawi resistance movement, the Polisario Front. It quickly fell to be replaced by another military government headed by Col. Mohamed Khouna Ould Haidallah who gave up all claims to Western Sahara by renouncing sovereignty over its share of former Spanish Sahara. His regime was plagued by attempted coups. In 1984 he was deposed by Col. Maaouya Ould Sid'Ahmed Taya, who relaxed the political climate somewhat, without relinquishing military control. Multi-party elections were held in 1992 and again in 1997, both won by Taya. A group of serving and retired Army officers launched a bloody but unsuccessful coup attempt on 8 June 2003. The leaders of the attempted coup were never caught. Presidential election, took place on 7 November 2003. Incumbent President Maaouya Ould Sid'Ahmed Taya won re-election with 67.02% of the popular vote, according to the official figures.

On 3 August 2005, a military coup led by Colonel Ely Ould Mohamed Vall ended Maaouya Ould Sid'Ahmed Taya's twenty-one years of rule. On that day, the Mauritanian military, including members of the presidential guard, seized control of key points in the capital of Nouakchott. They took advantage of President Taya's attendance at the funeral of Saudi King Fahd to organize the coup, which took place without loss of life. The officers, calling themselves the Military Council for Justice and Democracy, released the following statement: "The national armed forces and security forces have unanimously decided to put a definitive end to the oppressive activities of the defunct authority, which our people have suffered from during the past years." The Military Council later issued another statement naming Colonel Vall as President and director of the national police force, the *Sûreté Nationale*. Applauded by the Mauritanian people, but cautiously watched by the international community, the coup was generally accepted. The military *junta* organized elections within the promised two year timeline.

In a referendum on 26 June 2006, Mauritanians overwhelmingly (97%) approved a new constitution which limited the duration of a president's stay in office. The leader of the junta, Col. Vall, promised to abide by the referendum and relinquish power peacefully. Mauritania's establishment of relations with the State of Israel – it was one of only three Arab states to recognize Israel – was maintained by the new regime, despite widespread criticism from the opposition, who viewed it as a legacy of the Taya regime's attempts to curry favour with the West.

The first fully democratic Presidential election since 1960 occurred on 11 March 2007. The election brought about the final transfer of power from military to civilian rule. It was won in a second round of voting by Sidi Ould Cheikh Abdallahi, with Ahmed Ould Daddah a close second. But just over a year later there was another coup, in 2008. The head of the Presidential Guards took over the president's palace and units of the army surrounded a key state building in the capital Nouakchott on 6 August 2008, a day after 48 lawmakers from the ruling party resigned. The army surrounded the state television building after the president sacked two senior officers, including the head of the presidential guards. The President, the Prime Minister and the Minister of Internal Affairs were arrested.

The coup was organized by General Mohamed Ould Abdel Aziz, former Chief of Staff of the Mauritanian Army and head of the Presidential Guard, whom the president had just dismissed. Mauritania's Presidential spokesman, Abdoulaye Mamadouba, said President Sidi Ould Cheikh Abdallahi, Prime Minister Yahya Ould Ahmed Waghf and the Interior Minister were arrested by renegade Senior Mauritanian army officers, unknown troops and a group of generals, and were held under house arrest at the presidential palace in Nouakchott. `Abd Al-`Aziz had since the coup insisted that there be organized new presidential elections to replace Abdellahi, but was forced to reschedule them due to internal and international opposition. However, in the second quarter of 2009, the junta negotiated an understanding with some opposition figures as well as international parties, which dramatically changed the situation. Abdellahi formally resigned, under protest. The resignation paved the way for the election of military strongman Muhammad Ould `Abd Al-`Aziz as civilian president, on 18 July, by a 52% majority.

## Niger

For its first fourteen years as an independent state, Niger was run by a single-party civilian regime under the presidency of Hamani Diori. In 1974, a combination of devastating drought and accusations of rampant corruption resulted in a coup d'état that overthrew the Diori regime. Col. Seyni Kountché and a small military group ruled the country until Kountché's death in 1987. He was succeeded by his Chief of Staff, Col. Ali Saibou, who released political prisoners, liberalized some of Niger's laws and policies, promulgated a new constitution, and created a one-party Republic. However, Saibou's efforts to control political reforms failed in the face of trade union and student demands for a multi-party democratic system. The Saibou regime acquiesced to these demands by the end of 1990.

A national peace conference was convened in July 1991 to prepare the way for the adoption of a new constitution, the holding of free and fair elections, and development of a plan for a transition government. A transitional government was duly installed in November 1991 to manage the affairs of state until the institutions of the new constitution were put in place in April 1993. The results of the January 1995 parliamentary election led to governmental paralysis. Col. Ibrahim Baré Maïnassara seized the opportunity to overthrow the government in January 1996. He had yet a new constitution drafted and in July 1996 organized a presidential election. He stood as candidate. While voting was still going on, he replaced the electoral commission with a new one which lost no time in declaring him winner.

Three years later, on 9 April 1999, Baré was killed in a coup led by Maj. Daouda Malam Wanké. Wanké established a transitional National Reconciliation Council to oversee the drafting of yet another constitution with a French-style semi-presidential system. Presidential elections were held in November 1999 and were won by Mamadou Tandja. In August 2002, serious unrest within the military occurred in Niamey, Diffa, and Nguigmi, but the government was able to restore order within several days. President Mamadou Tandja was re-elected in December 2004. From 2007 to 2008, the Tuareg in northern Niger revolted for the second time, worsening economic prospects and shutting down political progress.

On 26 May 2009, President Tandja dissolved parliament after the country's constitutional court ruled against plans to hold a referendum on whether to allow him a third term in office. He called a referendum to adopt a new constitution. The new constitution contained no presidential term limits even though the existing Constitution explicitly prohibited amendment of the two-term limit, even by referendum. This touched off a political struggle between Tandja, trying to extend his term-limited authority beyond 2009, and his opponents who demanded that he step down at the end of his second term in December 2009.

Thrice the Constitutional Court of Niger ruled that any such referendum would be unconstitutional. Tandja reacted by simply dissolving the Court, claiming it lacked the competence to deal with such matters. Tandja then also dissolved the National Assembly which was also opposed to his referendum plan. By June of 2009, Tandja had effectively dismantled both the judicial and legislative branches of government. Public protests and trade union strikes against the proposed referendum continued. Amidst all these protests Tandja proceeded with his referendum. The new constitution was passed, giving Tandja sweeping and enormous powers that practically made him a dictator and guaranteed his indefinite stay in power.

ECOWAS reacted by suspending Niger's membership of the Organization and imposing sanctions against the country. Both the EU and the US also reacted by suspending budgetary support and financial assistance. But Tandja was defiant. In 1999 the military had gained the public's trust when its intervention (the coup by Major Malam Daouda Wanké that overthrew Col Ibrahim Baré Maïnassara) played a key role in establishing a democratic government, ending the first Tuareg revolt and bringing stability to the country for the first time in decades. With this in mind, various stakeholders publicly called upon the military to stop obeying Tanja. But speaking through its spokesperson, Colonel Goukoye Abdoulkarim, the military declared its continued neutrality in political matters. "Mindful of national unity, the defence forces do not serve partisan interests. Duty-bound to be neutral and reserved, the armed forces cannot as such be associated with any political debate, or be involved in destabilizing actions." In reality the military wanted to test the tenacity of the country's civil institutions before intervening. By February 2010, Tandja's new despotic government was firmly in place and the country was in the throes of a humanitarian crisis.

On February 18, 2010, a faction of Niger's army known as the *Conseil Suprême pour la Restoration de la Démocratie* (CSRD), Supreme Council for the Restoration of Democracy, led by Col Salou Djibo and Djibrilla Hamidou Hima staged a military coup by storming the presidential residence and deposing Mamadou Tandja. The coup was immediately condemned by much of the international community. But the military takeover won the praises of a significant majority of Niger's public and various stakeholders. The junta immediately took steps to reassure the public and the international community that it intended to restore the country's democracy and constitutional order. It appointed a civilian as Prime Minister and announced that no member of the junta, or the interim government, will be permitted to run in the upcoming presidential election. The election was billed for January 20111.

## Nigeria

The 1966 coup attempt by Ibo-led army dissidents failed when loyalists led by General Ironsi prevailed. The Prime Minister Abubakar Tafawa Belewa was killed in the coup attempt. The rump of the Federal Cabinet was handed over to General Ironsi who proceeded to set up a Supreme Military Council with himself as Chairman. Ironsi himself was killed in a Hausa-inspired counter coup of July that year. General Yakubu Gowon was put in power. A pogrom against the Ibos eventually led to a three-year civil war pitting the Ibos who declared secession from the rest of Nigeria.

General Gowon, the victor of the Nigeria civil war was ousted from power in 1975 in a coup by General Murtala Ramat Mohammed who perished just months afterwards in an abortive coup led by Col Dimka. Murtala was succeeded by another soldier, General Abdulsalam who promised a return of power to civilians. Abdulsalam organized elections and handed power to a democratically elected civilian, Shehu Shagari. But Shagari did not last as he was overthrown in 1983 by Muhammadu Buhari, himself overthrown in 1985 in a coup by General Ibrahim Babangida. In 1990 there was a failed coup by Col. Gideon Orkar.

Babangida was ousted by General Sani Abacha who died in power in 1998. Power then reverted to civilian under Obasanjo, a former military officer, and then to Yar'adua who died in office in early 2010. His Vice President, Jonathan Ebelle Goodluck, took over. He ran for the presidential election of January 2011 and won.

## Rwanda

In 1960, the Belgian government agreed to hold democratic local elections in Ruanda-Urundi. Hutu representatives were elected by the Hutu majority. This precipitous change in the power equation threatened the centuries-old system by which Tutsi superiority had been maintained through monarchy. An effort to create an independent Ruanda-Urundi with Tutsi-Hutu power sharing failed, largely due to escalating violence. The Belgian government, with UN urging, decided to divide Ruanda-Urundi into two separate countries,

Rwanda and Burundi. Each had elections in 1961 in preparation for independence.

In 1961, Rwandans voted, by referendum and with the support of the Belgian colonial government, to abolish the Tutsi monarchy. A republic was established. Dominique Mbonyumutwa was named the first President of the transitional government. Between 1961 and 1962, Tutsi guerrilla groups staged attacks into Rwanda from neighbouring countries. Rwandan Hutu-based troops responded and thousands were killed in the clashes. On July 1, 1962, Belgium, with UN supervision, granted full independence to the two countries. Rwanda was created as a republic governed by the majority Party of the Hutu Emancipation Movement (Parmehutu), which had gained full control of national politics by this time.

In 1963, a Tutsi guerrilla invasion into Rwanda from Burundi unleashed another anti-Tutsi backlash by the Hutu government in Rwanda. In response, a previous economic union between Rwanda and Burundi was dissolved and tensions between the two countries worsened. Rwanda became a Hutu-dominated one-party state. Gregoire Kayibanda, founder of Parmehutu was the first President from 1962 to 1973 when he was overthrown in a coup by General Juvenal Habyarimana. Habyarimana claimed that Kayibanda's government was ineffective and riddled with favouritism. He was in power from 1973 until 1994 when he was killed.

In 1990 the Rwandan Patriotic Front (RPF), a rebel group, composed mostly of Tutsi refugees, staged yet another invasion of Rwanda this time from Uganda in the north. In the ensuing Rwandan Civil War, the Hutu regime had the support of Francophone nations of Africa and France itself, while the Tutsi RPF had the support of Uganda. This war greatly exacerbated the ethnic tensions in the Rwanda. Despite continuing ethnic strife, including the displacement of large numbers of Hutu in the north by the rebels and periodic localized extermination of Tutsi to the south, pressure on the government of Habyarimana resulted in a cease-fire in 1993 and the preliminary implementation of the Arusha Accords.

On 6 April 1994 President Habyarimana and the Burundian President were killed when Habyarimana's plane was shot down near Kigali Airport. The shooting down of the plane served as the trigger for the genocide that followed. In the course of the next few months the Hutu majority in Rwanda organized and implemented the mass slaughter of the Tutsi minority. Hundreds of thousands of Rwanda's Tutsis and Hutu political moderates were killed. Over the course of approximately 100 days, from the assassination of Habyarimana on 6 April through mid-July, at least 500.000 people were killed. Estimates of the death toll have ranged between 500.000 and 1.000.000, or as much as 20% of the total population of the country.

The assassination of Habyarimana was the proximate cause of the mass killings of Tutsis and pro-peace Hutus. They were carried out primarily by two Hutu militias associated with political parties: the *Interahamwe* and the *Impuzamugambi*. The genocide was directed by a Hutu power group known as the *Akazu*. The killing also marked the end of the peace agreement that was to end the war. The Tutsi RPF restarted their offensive, eventually defeating the Rwandese army and seizing control of the country.

About two million people fled from Rwanda, to Burundi, Tanzania, Uganda, and for the most part Zaire. After the victory of the RPF, the size of United Nations Assistance Mission for Rwanda was increased to its full strength, remaining in Rwanda until 8 March 1996. In October 1996, an uprising by the ethnic Tutsi *Banyamulenge* people in eastern Zaire marked the beginning of the First Congo War. It led to a return of more than 600,000 people to Rwanda during the last two weeks of November. This massive repatriation was followed at the end of December 1996 by the return of 500,000 more from Tanzania after they were ejected by the Tanzanian government. Various successor organizations to the Hutu militants operated in eastern DR Congo until May 2009.

*São Tomé and Príncipe*
In 1995, young officers carried out a coup in protest against the country's poverty. Power was handed back to the civilian government

following successful mediation by the Angolan government. The country's 900-strong military again seized power on 17 July 2003, arguing that the country was politically unstable and economically beset with difficulties. The coup makers overthrew President Fradique de Menezes, elected in 1991. They put in place a 'military junta of national salvation' to run the affairs of the tiny Island country. Nigeria condemned the coup in strong terms and called for the restoration of the legitimate government of the country.

## Sierra Leone

In 1967 President Margai was overthrown by Lt Col Juxon-Smith. Power was eventually returned to civilian rule under President Siaka Stevens. But in 1978 Stevens was overthrown by Major General Joseph Momoh. In 1992 Momoh was overthrown by 26-year old Captain Valentine Strasser. In response to international pressure Strasser organized in February 1996 multiparty elections which were won by Kabbah. On 25 May 1997, the barely sixteen months old democratically elected government of President Ahmed Tejan Kabbah was overthrown by Major General Paul Koromah. Koromah gave as his excuse for ousting Kabbah, the latter's alleged failure to provide adequate financial support for the army and his alleged tribalism, and questioned the legitimacy of the Kabbah government.

The coup was condemned worldwide and not a single country recognized the usurper government. On 8 October 1997 the UN Security Council adopted Resolution 1132 imposing sanctions on the regime, including an international ban on the supply of arms and petroleum products. In February 1998, the Nigerian-led West African intervention force, ECOMOG, stormed Freetown and occupied it on behalf of exiled President Kabbah until his triumphant return on 10 March 1998. The usurpers had been in power for ten months. They were arrested, tried for treason, convicted and executed.

## Somalia

An Italian UN mandated, then trustee, Somalia had the opportunity to gain experience in political education and self-government. In 1948, the British who held British Somaliland as a protectorate 'returned' the *Haud* (an important Somali grazing area) and the *Ogaden* to Ethiopia, based on a treaty they signed in 1897 in which the British ceded Somali territory to the Ethiopian Emperor Menelik in exchange for his help against plundering by Somali clans. Britain included the proviso that the Somali nomads would retain their autonomy, but Ethiopia immediately claimed sovereignty over them.

Britain also granted administration of the almost exclusively Somali-inhabited Northern Frontier District (NFD) to Kenyan nationalists despite an informal plebiscite demonstrating the overwhelming desire of the region's population to join the newly formed Somali Republic. A referendum was held in neighbouring Djibouti (then known as French Somaliland) in 1958, on the eve of Somalia's independence in 1960, to decide whether or not to join the Somali Republic or to remain with France. The referendum turned out in favour of a continued association with France, largely due to a combined yes vote by the sizable Afar ethnic group and resident Europeans. Djibouti finally gained its independence from France in 1977 and Hassan Gouled Aptidon, a French-groomed Somali who campaigned for a yes vote in the referendum of 1958, eventually wound up as Djibouti's first president (1977–1991).

British Somaliland became independent on June 26, 1960, and the former Italian Somaliland followed suit five days later. On July 1, 1960, the two territories united to form the Somali Republic, albeit within boundaries drawn up by Italy and Britain. On July 20, 1961 and through a popular referendum, the Somali people ratified a new constitution, which was first drafted in 1960. In 1967, Muhammad Haji Ibrahim Egal became Prime Minister and later the President of the autonomous Somaliland region in north-western Somalia. In late 1969, following the assassination of President Shermarke, a military government assumed power in a coup d'état led by Major General Salaad Gabeyre Kediye, General Siad Barre and Chief of Police Jama Korshel. Barre became President and Korshel vice-president.

It was in July 1976 when the real dictatorship of the Somali military commenced until the fall of the military government in January 1991. In 1977 and 1978, Somalia unsuccessfully invaded its neighbour Ethiopia in the Ogaden War, to unite the Somali lands that had been partitioned by the former colonial powers, and to win the right of self-determination for ethnic Somalis in those territories. By 1978, the moral authority of the Somali government had collapsed. Many Somalis had become disillusioned with life under military dictatorship and the regime was weakened further in the 1980s as the Cold War drew to a close and Somalia's strategic importance was diminished. The government became increasingly totalitarian, and resistance movements, encouraged by Ethiopia, sprang up across the country, eventually leading to the Somali Civil War.

In 1991 President Barre was ousted by combined northern and southern clan-based forces, all of whom were backed and armed by Ethiopia. And following a meeting of the Somali National Movement and northern clans' elders, the northern former British portion of the country declared its independence as Somaliland in May 1991. Although it is de facto independent and relatively stable compared to the tumultuous south, Somaliland has not been recognised de jure by any foreign government.

Mohamed Farrah Aidid saw UNOSOM II as a threat to his power and in June 1993 his militia attacked Pakistani troops, attached to UNOSOM II in Mogadishu inflicting over 80 casualties. Fighting escalated until 19 American troops and more than 1,000 Somalis were killed in a raid in Mogadishu during October 1993. The UN withdrew Operation United Shield on 3 March 1995, having suffered significant casualties, and with the rule of government still not restored. In August 1996, Aidid was killed in Mogadishu.

In 2006, the Islamic Courts Union (ICU), an Islamist organization, assumed control of much of the southern part of the country and promptly imposed Shari'a law. The Transitional Federal Government sought to re-establish its authority. With the assistance of Ethiopian troops, African Union peacekeepers and air support by the United States, it managed to drive out the rival ICU and solidify its rule.

Following this defeat, the Islamic Courts Union splintered into several different factions. Some of the more radical elements, including Al-Shabaab, regrouped to continue their insurgency against the TFG and to oppose Ethiopian military presence in Somalia. Throughout 2007 and 2008, Al-Shabaab scored military victories, seizing control of key towns and ports in both central and southern Somalia. At the end of 2008, the group had captured Baidoa but not Mogadishu. By January 2009, Al-Shabaab and other militias had managed to force the Ethiopian troops to withdraw from the country, leaving behind an under-equipped African Union peacekeeping force to assist the Transitional Federal Government's troops.

On 29 December 2008, Abdullahi Yusuf Ahmed announced before a united parliament in Baidoa his resignation as President of Somalia. Over the next few months, a new President was elected from amongst the more moderate Islamists, and Omar Abdirashid Ali Sharmarke, the son of slain former President Abdirashid Ali Sharmarke, was selected as the nation's new Prime Minister. In March 2009, Somalia's newly established coalition government announced that it would re-implement Shari'a as the nation's official judicial system. However, conflict continued in the southern and central parts of the country between government troops and extremist Islamist militants with links to al-Qaeda.

*South African Homelands (apartheid era)*

During the apartheid era the white government carved out four Black homelands (Bophuthatswana, Ciskei, Transkei and Venda) and granted them nominal 'independence'. No country in the world recognized any of the homelands as a sovereign state. The homelands lasted for about twenty years. Although none of them fulfilled the conditions for statehood under international law, each nevertheless had a government, which government in each case was overthrown by coup d'état.

## Bophuthatswana:

The area was set up as the only homeland for Tswana-speaking people in 1961. It was given nominal self-rule in 1971 and became nominally independent on 6 December 1977. For the first election shortly before independence, 48 seats in its 96-seat parliament were open, the remainder being reserved for appointed local chiefs. Kgosi Lucas Manyane Mangope became president after his *Democratic Party (DP)* gained the majority of them. Six seats were won by the *Seoposengwe Party (SP)*. Bophuthatswana's 'independence' was not recognized by any government other than those of South Africa and Transkei, the first homeland to gain nominal independence. In addition, it was later internally recognized by the two additional countries within the TVBC-system, Ciskei and Venda.

Despite its official isolation, however, the government in Mmabatho managed to set up a trade mission in Tel Aviv, Israel, and conducted some business with neighbouring Botswana in an effort to sway attitudes; furthermore, Botswana agreed on "informal arrangements" short of official recognition in order to facilitate cross-border travel. Arguing in favour of independence, President Mangope claimed that the move would enable its population to negotiate with South Africa from a stronger position:

> "We would rather face the difficulties of administering a fragmented territory, the wrath of the outside world, and accusations of ill-informed people. It's the price we are prepared to pay for being masters of our own destiny. ... [A]t last we are no longer helplessly at the mercy of the arbitrary arrogance of those who until this hour trampled our human dignity into the dust."

The General Assembly denounced the declaration of the so-called "independence" of Bophuthatswana and declared it totally invalid. United Nations Secretary-General Kurt Waldheim stated that he "strongly deplored" the establishment of "another so-called independent tribal homeland in pursuance of the discredited policies of apartheid," and in resolution A/RES/32/105N, passed on 14

December 1977, the United Nations General Assembly linked Bophuthatswana's "so-called 'independence'" to South Africa's "stubborn pursuit" of its policies, and called upon all governments to "deny any form of recognition to the so-called 'independent' bantustans." During a parliamentary debate in Great Britain on 6 December 1977, the Secretary of State replied in the negative when asked "whether Her Majesty's Government intend to recognise travel documents issued by the authorities of [...] Bophuthatswana for the purpose of admitting visitors to the United Kingdom."

While the majority of news reports echoed these official declarations, there were others which opined that Western critics should "suspend judgment for a time," and despite its generally critical stance on South Africa's policies, *Time* magazine wrote that Bophuthatswana had "considerable economic potential" with an expected $30 million a year coming from mining revenues.

On 10 February 1988 Rocky Malabane-Metsing of the *People's Progressive Party (PPP)* became the President of Bophuthatswana for one day when he took over the government through a military coup. He accused Mangope of corruption and charged that the recent election had been rigged in the government's favour. A statement by the defence force said "serious and disturbing matters of great concern" had emerged, citing Mr. Mangope's close association with a multimillionaire Soviet émigré. During the subsequent invasion of the South African Defence Force, Mangope was reinstated and continued his presidency. PW Botha, president of South Africa at the time, justified the reinstatement by saying that "[t]he South African Government is opposed in principle to the obtaining of power by violence."

In 1990, during a second coup in which an estimated 50,000 protesters demanded the president's resignation over his handling of the economy, the New York Times reported that seven people had been killed and 450 wounded "after police officers in armoured cars fired their rifles into the crowds and used tear gas and rubber bullets." After Mangope had asked for help from the South African government, he declared a state of emergency and cut telephone links to the territory "for political reasons," claiming that "normal laws had become inadequate." The United Nations' Human Rights Watch put the number of protesters at 150,000.

In the beginning of 1994 with South Africa heading for democratic elections, Mangope resisted reincorporation into South Africa. Forty people were wounded when Bophuthatswana Defence Force troops opened fire on striking civil servants. Mangope took an increasingly hard-line stance, rejected Independent Electoral Commission chairman Judge Johann Kriegler's plea for free political activity in the territory, and fired the staff of the Bophuthatswana Broadcasting Corporation, closing down two television stations and three radio stations.

The white supremacist group Afrikaner Weerstandsbeweging (AWB) took the opportunity to move in and try to restore the apartheid status quo, but was humiliated in early March when, in the presence of photojournalists and a TV crew, uniformed members of the AWB on an armed incursion to the Mmabatho/Mafikeng area shot at people alongside the road, injuring and killing many. They themselves were shot at by members of the Bophuthatswana Defence Force (BDF) and the Police and forced to retreat. Three wounded AWB members were shot dead at point blank range by Ontlametse Bernstein Menyatsoe of the BDF while retreating. These killings effectively spelt the end of white military opposition to democratic reforms. Mangope was replaced by an interim government.

### Ciskei:

The Ciskei became a separate administrative region in 1961. In 1972 it was declared self-governing under the rule of Chief Justice Mabandla and then Lennox Sebe. In 1978 it became a single-party state under the rule of Lennox Sebe and in 1981 it became the fourth homeland to be declared independent by the South African government and its residents lost their South African citizenship. Like the case with other Bantustans its independence was not recognised by the international community. Sebe was deposed in

169

1990 by Brigadier Oupa Gqozo, who ruled as a dictator. The ANC pressed strongly for the Homelands to be reincorporated into South Africa. This was opposed by Gqozo.

On 7 September 1992 the Ciskei Defence Force fired into a crowd of ANC members demanding the removal of Gqozo. Twenty-eight people were killed and hundreds injured in the Bisho massacre outside the sports stadium in Bisho. Gqozo refused to participate in the multiracial negotiations and initially threatened to boycott the first multiracial elections. This became unsustainable and in March 1994, the police then mutinied, prompting Gqozo to resign on 22 March. Ciskei and all of the other homelands were reincorporated into South Africa on 27 April 1994, after the first post-apartheid elections. Along with Transkei, it became part of the new Eastern Cape Province. Its capital became the capital of the Eastern Cape Province.

**Transkei:**

In 1987, there was a coup d'état in the Transkei led by General Bantu Holomisa, the then leader of the Transkei Defence Force. The coup ousted from power Prime Minister George Matanzima, 68, who had banished to the village his brother Kaiser D. Matanzima, 71, the former President, who had led Transkei to "independence" from South Africa in 1976 and who had retired as head of state in 1985. Holomisa became head of state of the Transkei following the coup. Three years later, in 1990, he survived a coup attempt. Those who carried out the failed coup were arrested and executed without trial.

Before 1976 Transkei formed part of the Republic of South Africa. It was granted a limited degree of self-rule in 1963 and then 'independence' in 1976 in terms of the Status of Transkei Act 100 of 1976 (RSA). That Act gave the Legislative Assembly of the Transkei power to adopt a Constitution for the territory, which it did and it came into effect on the day of 'independence', 26 October 1976. On 24 September 1987 it was announced that the then Prime Minister, Chief George Matanzima, had fled the country and that eight Cabinet Ministers had been forced to resign by the Transkei Defence Force "when it came to light that corruption had occurred in the highest levels of Government and commissions of inquiry then sitting had revealed the evidence of such corruption."

At about noon on 30 December 1987, Bantu Holomisa, as Commander of the Transkei Defence Force, announced over the National Radio that martial law had been declared and the Constitution suspended. Soldiers under his command moved into the centre of the capital (then spelt 'Umtata'), helicopters flew over the city and army vehicles moved through the streets declaring the imposition of 'Military Rule'. Holomisa also announced that the country would be run 'in the interim' by an 'interim Government' consisting of a Military Council supported by an appointed Council of Ministers. Although hundreds of heavily armed soldiers and police patrolled the streets of Mthatha, manned roadblocks, guarded key installations and raided the homes of politicians, no one was arrested or placed under house arrest. Members of the Cabinet were instructed to leave their offices, remove their possessions from their ministerial houses and return the Government vehicles in their possession. The Public Service continued to perform its functions and the border posts between the country and the Republic of South Africa remained open.

On 31 December martial law was lifted, there being no civil unrest and no apparent threat of such unrest. On 5 January 1988, Decree 1 inter alia, dissolved the already suspended Parliament, established a Military Council and a Council of Ministers to govern the country until restoration of civilian rule, empowered the President to make laws by decree for the peace, order and good government of Transkei, declared the courts incompetent to inquire into or to pronounce upon the validity of any decree, and directed that all courts and commissions lawfully established in terms of the existing laws shall continue to exercise jurisdiction and have the powers that they exercised and had hitherto. From that date until its re-integration into South Africa the Transkei was governed in terms of that decree.

## Venda:

Venda was declared self-governing on 1 February 1973 and on 13 September 1979, it was declared independent by the South African government. Its independence, like that of the other Homelands, was not recognized by the international community. Venda was initially a series of non-contiguous territories in the Transvaal, with one main part and one main exclave. Its capital, formerly at Sibasa, was moved to Thohoyandou. Prior to independence it was expanded to form one contiguous territory, with a total land area of 6,807 km². The Homeland was cut off from neighbouring Zimbabwe by the Madimbo corridor, patrolled by South African troops, to the north, and from nearby Mozambique by the Kruger National Park. The first President of Venda, Patrick Mphephu, was also a chief of the Venda people. His successor, Frank Ravele, was overthrown in a military coup in 1990, after which the territory was ruled by the Council of National Unity. Venda was re-absorbed into South Africa on 27 April 1994.

*Sudan*

In 1958, the Prime Minister, Abdallah Khalil, an ex-Brigadier, requested his old friend, General Abboud, to take over power temporarily and rescue the government from a host of problems which it could not cope with. Abboud carried out Khalid's request to suspend Parliament and ban political parties; but he proceeded to replace the government by a military junta that became entrenched in power. When Nimeri seized power in 1969 and a counter coup against him in 1971 failed, the leader of the coup that had lasted three days were given swift 'trials', sentenced and executed. In 1989, General al Bashir seized power from the democratically elected government of Sadiq al Mahdi and his Umma (People's) Party. Twenty-three years on, Bashir is still in power.

*Uganda*

Uganda gained independence from Britain in 1962, maintaining its Commonwealth membership. Shortly after independence, the differences between the northern and southern parts of the country surfaced. The northern pastoralists felt overshadowed by the southern agriculturists. The Christians had once been preferred by the British authorities. They now chaffed under the increasing influence of the Muslims. The first post-independence election was held in 1962. It was won by an alliance between the Uganda People's Congress (UPC) and Kabaka Yekka (KY). UPC and KY formed the first post-independence government with Milton Obote as executive Prime Minister, the Buganda Kabaka (King) Edward Muteesa II holding the largely ceremonial position of President and William Wilberforce Nadiope, the Kyabazinga (Paramount Chief) of Busoga, as Vice President. The north/south dichotomy and tension in the country was compounded in 1964 when the military staged a coup d'état demanding promotions and higher pay. The coup was crushed with the aid of British troops. But Obote eventually granted the military their demands in exchange for their constant support. For the security of himself and his regime, he decided to choose a low-ranking soldier, Idi Amin, to groom as his protégé. The illiterate Idi Amin quickly rose through the ranks and took command of the military.

In 1966, there was a power struggle between the Obote-led government and King Muteesa. The UPC-dominated Parliament changed the constitution and removed the ceremonial president and vice president. In 1967, a new constitution proclaimed Uganda a republic and abolished the traditional kingdoms. Without first calling elections, Obote was declared the executive President. Obote was on an official visit to northern Uganda, when the government issued a vote of no confidence against him. He invited Amin to stage a coup d'état against the very government he, Obote, was head of. Amin complied. Obote was firmly placed in power. Obote dissolved his government, passed a new constitution, and instituted martial law to deal with any resistance.

Within a few years, however, Obote felt increasingly insecure as several attempts were made on his life. He became very suspicious of Amin. In 1970 Obote placed Amin under house arrest for some financial misdemeanour and in 1971 while on a diplomatic mission abroad ordered the arrest of Amin and his troops. But word leaked to Amin and he struck first. He staged a coup d'état, deposing Obote who fled into exile in Tanzania.

Amin ruled the country with an iron fist. For 8 years there was a bloody reign of terror and an estimated 300,000 Ugandans lost their lives. A border scuffle between Uganda and Tanzania led to war in 1979. Tanzanian troops, aided by Ugandan exiles, fought their way through to Kampala, capital of Ugandan, deposing Amin who fled into permanent exile in Saudi Arabia where he died many years later.

An interim government was established under the Ugandan National Liberation Front (UNLF) which spent its time bickering over policy. In the meantime various insurgency groups continued to consolidate in the field. One such group was led by a Colonel Yoweri Museveni. The group, soon to be known as the NRA, had broken away from Amin's army and had aided the Tanzanian forces in his expulsion. Another group was Andrew Kayiira's Federal Democratic Movement (FDM) and still another group was that of John Nkwaanga. In 1980 the UNLF interim government was overthrown in a coup d'état. Obote returned to Uganda and ran for the presidential election that was held in December that year.

According to some accounts, when the rival Democratic Party was declared winner, Obote's loyal troops 'recounted' the votes in favour of Obote. Obote became the President of Uganda for the second time. He was soon at loggerheads with Museveni's insurgency group which declared itself the NRA claiming to be fighting for the common people and for fair elections. Since the late 1984 unrest was gradually building up in the Ugandan army due to the inability of the army to win the 'bush war' against the NRA and other insurgency groups. In 1985 the unrest came to a climax. Obote ordered the arrest of his top military advisers. Their reaction was predictable. Bazilio Olara-Okello and Tito Lutwa Okello staged a successful coup.

Obote was overthrown for the second time in his political career and for the second time he went into exile, this time permanently, to Tanzania and then to Zambia where he eventually died many years later.

Gen Tito Okello proceeded to rule through a Military Council. The coup gave heart to Museveni's National Resistance Army (NRA) insurgency group. It re-organised and eventually become a force at par with the government army. Okello's Military Council then invited the NRA to join them in forming a government. Musevi, "steeped in Machiavellian politics and military doctrine", did; but he lost no time in turning and ousting the Okello military government in 1986. Shortly after Museveni came to power, the other insurgency groups gave up their fight. But several of their officers and men were arrested and detained. Many simply disappeared without ever being heard from again. Twenty-five years on, Museveni is still in power in Uganda.

# Chapter 12

## Epilogue: Neo-patrimonial Governance and Revolutionary Overthrow of Governments in Africa[81]

Many African states continue to rely on centralized and highly personalized forms of government. They lack democratic institutions and have fallen into a pattern of corruption, a pattern of governance based on personal rule and ethnicity, and a pattern of gross human rights abuses. The African ruler tends to see himself as ruler for life. In order to cling on to power indefinitely he has no scruples manipulating elections and diverting the military and police to focus on protecting him, his family and his regime. He has no scruples manipulating ethnicity, manipulating the constitution, and harassing and torturing dissidents and political opponents. It is very sad that most African militaries exist to protect the ruler and to serve and save his regime rather than serve the national interest and protect citizens and the country. Overdue stay in power is one of the sources of conflicts in Africa and a key contributory factor to corruption, graft and patronage. It is significant that African countries that have rulers who have been in power for decades are among the most corrupt and the least developed in the world.

In Africa, participation of citizens in the government of their country is more abstract than real. The ruler continues to be overbearing and to wield excessive power. The concept of separation of powers has little meaning in many African states. There is only one office and one power that matters – that of the ruler. All else is mere decoration. The ruler issues decrees that override constitutional provisions, parliamentary deliberations, and court decisions. The

---

[81] Anyangwe C, 'Good Governance, Democracy and Corruption in Africa', in: R Simigiannis & C Letlojane (ed.), *Human Rights Theories and Practices*, HURISA, Johannesburg, 2001, p. 215.

legislature is a mere rubber stamp, the judiciary a dependent and timid organ, and both lack the power to control executive excesses. The ruler uses and controls the national purse as if it were his private bank account.

## The rise of the neo-patrimonial state in Africa

The values of democracy and good governance are yet to find fertile soil in most of Africa. The political climate is inhospitable to democracy in part due to bad governance, the culture of authoritarianism, and endless conflicts. Elections have since become an expensive nonsensical ritual. Conflicts are themselves the direct product of varied factors. These include over-centralization of political and economic power, personalization of forms of government, suppression of political pluralism, political monopoly and its attendant corruption and abuse of power, 'winner-takes-all' form of political victory, lack of respect for human rights, lack of accountability, oppression, and the domination and oppression of others by the dominant identity.

And yet the attainment of independence held out promise of democracy and good governance. Indeed, African freedom fighters did not fight to replace alien oppressors with indigenous ones. Independence was meant to usher in an era of freedom, democracy, justice, peace and development. The masses therefore legitimately expected better days ahead. This expectation quickly turned out to be an evanescent hope. The promise of independence soon became a mere mirage. More than half a century after decolonization, it is still not yet *uhuru*. Here and there pirates have taken control of the state and the continent appears helpless and purposeless. Personal dictatorships, one-party dictatorships, military dictatorships, a warlord culture, and a species of governance anchored on the gun and ethnicity have since emerged and taken root in many countries.

A first trend, at once insidious and invidious, consisted in the establishment of government by the personal rule of one man and his immediate political and tribal coterie. The ruler in effect hijacked the state. He converted it into his personal fiefdom, driven by corruption and patron-client relations. He became well ensconced in the self-same State House vacated by the evicted colonizer. He lost no time in embracing the authoritarian nature of colonial governance, complete with its trappings and illiberal laws as well as its patronizing and self-serving logic. State apparatus, state power, and state resources became instruments in the distribution of patrimony, patronage and graft to relatives, tribesmen, friends and political confederates. The ruler's complete control over and manipulation of the military and police ensured his continuing hold on power, albeit tenuous.

In Africa the ruler bestrides the state like a colossus. He lives in sinful splendour and arrogance, and revels in opulence. Meanwhile the generality of the people cringe in terror and gnash their teeth in abject poverty and disease. Each time word of the rot in the regime filters out the regime's spin doctors immediately swing to action peddling the myth of the ruler's personal probity.[82] The familiar line of this myth is that the ruler himself is an upright and well-meaning individual with the country's interest deeply embedded in his heart. According to the myth the only problem is that the virtuous ruler is surrounded by corrupt ministers and advisers, and/or is evilly influenced by a villainous wife. As proof of his cleanness and integrity the ruler would then make a show of clearing the corruption around him.

One or two scapegoats are identified and sacrificed. In order to give an appearance of credence to this superficial and token exercise, an investigation would be promised and even instituted. But at that point the ruler's mighty war against corruption comes to an end. Prosecutions, if any, are selective and episodic. Arrestees are merely put through the motion of a court 'trial' and then sent to jail on the ruler's orders and at his pleasure. Corrupt officials who are said to have been dismissed are in reality merely put in the cooler for a short while before being brought out and given some other lucrative

---

[82] S McCarthy, *Africa: The Challenge of Transformation*, London, 1994, p. 106.

position in the next series of appointments by the ruler. Other corrupt officials are merely shifted, without even the pretence of demotion, to other juicy posts in government. The question never arises of the ruler taking responsibility for the deleterious conduct of his appointees.

Regimes have found it triply useful to peddle this myth of the upright ruler. The myth has the effect of shielding the ruler from political censure, opprobrium, and popular animosity and therefore possible insurrection. Further, the myth encourages citizens in the false belief that they are governed by an honest ruler, the so-called 'father of the nation', who has their best interest at heart. Citizens then keep on tolerating the failings, crimes and other shortcomings of the ruler in the misplaced belief that he will change and eventually deliver on the promised Eldorado. Finally the myth deludes international cooperating partners into believing or into pretending to believe that they are dealing with an essentially legitimate and honest regime.

In the lexicon of political scientists, this emergent African system of rule is termed the neo-patrimonial government. Its rise in Africa signalled the collapse of western-type constitutions bequeathed by the departed colonial powers.

"Westminster-style democratic leadership, based on open debate and an open electoral process, which was inherited from the colonial masters at the time of decolonization, has disappeared almost everywhere in Africa and given way to different and often less democratic patterns of leadership."[83]

The rise of the neo-patrimonial state in Africa makes a complete nonsense of the tested principle of separation of powers. Legislative assemblies ape the ruler, himself cynically imitating colonial administration. Judiciaries lack independence and dispense black justice. Gross human rights violations have become commonplace and go unchecked.

---

[83] Mazrui & Tidy, *Nationalism and New States in Africa*, Nairobi, 1984, p. 187.

# Continuing democracy and good governance deficit

The collapse of the Soviet Union in 1989 and the consequential ending of the cold war set in motion a wind of democratization which started blowing across Eastern Europe. By 1990 that good wind was lapping on the shores of Africa, adding to the mounting domestic pressure for democracy and political pluralism. Crusaders for democracy made bold to call for a second liberation of Africa – liberation from home grown oppressors. In country after country the masses, oppressed, hungry and angry as they were, took to the streets calling for 'change' and for effective participation in the governance of the country. They bore their naked chests and their wretched selves to the oppressor's bullets bought with taxpayers' money. Change looked inevitable. One after the other, Africa's rulers suddenly underwent a road-to-Damascus-like conversion to democracy. Or so it seemed. They began to speak about democracy and to extol its virtues with an Alice-in-Wonderland eloquence. For a while there was some let up in dictatorial terror.

But just as quickly as it had come, the wind of democratization also quickly abated. After finding out how the land lies, pro-democracy activists discovered to their utter dismay and discomfiture that African rulers had merely paid lip service to the idea of democracy, appropriated the idiom of democracy as a self-serving instrumental strategy. Not a single one of them bought into the idea of genuine political pluralism. There was no political willingness to embark on the road to democratization and a free society. In most states the regime in power had cunningly fostered overnight scores or hundreds of political parties which it then pointed to as evidence of political pluralism and 'democracy'.

At the same time also regimes cynically instigated and sponsored the tribalism of kinship corporations to re-surface under the thin disguise of political parties. The aim of this contemptuous strategy was to prevent the emergent political forces from coalescing and electorally defeating the incumbent ruler. By literally manufacturing and flooding the place with political parties the ruler also made sure that there was only a counterfeit political pluralism in place. By fostering so many political parties, the ruler, nurtured and cast in the mould of one-party orthodoxy, laid the groundwork for the eventual demonization of multi-party politics as a vehicle for ethnic friction and national fragmentation.

Not surprising therefore, a new discourse soon emerged in the continent. That discourse is a veiled advocacy of autocratic rule. It argues that there is no single one-size-fits-all model of democracy, that it is undemocratic to provide for presidential term limits, and that it is democratic and patriotic for a president to stay in power for as long as the people want him there. The new discourse further runs like this. African traditional system of governance is essentially democratic. It is even better because it is based on dialogue and consensus rather than the western confrontational system implied in the very idea of a political *opposition*. It took the West centuries to get to where it is today and much of what it is promoting is based on its own culture and civilization. Africa should not be stampeded or coerced into a system of governance out of character with the values of its traditions and civilization. Africa's urgent priorities are nation-building, the eradication of disease and poverty, the containment and prevention of HIV/AIDS, the development of the nation, and the 'fight' for a level international playing field. So in July 1990 the OAU Assembly of Heads of State and Government adopted a Declaration on the Political and Socio-Economic Situation in Africa and the Fundamental Changes Taking Place in the World. In that document Africa's Heads of State and Government declared:

> We … commit ourselves to the further democratization of our societies and to the consolidation of democratic institutions in our countries. We reaffirm the right of our countries to determine in all sovereignty, their system of democracy on the basis of their socio-cultural values, taking into account the realities of each of our countries and the necessity to ensure development and satisfy the basic needs of our people. We

therefore assert that democracy and development should go together and should be mutually reinforcing.

African political watchers interpreted the declaration as the response of Africa's esteemed rulers to the combined pressure by civil society and aid donors for democratization in the continent. This response denied that African states have not democratized and do not have democratic institutions. The declaration told a lie when it claimed that African states have put democratic institutions in place and have all along been democratizing. The document claimed that all that Africa needed in this regard was simply "to further democratise" and to continue with "the consolidation of democratic institutions". The declaration then sought to make a case for the Africanisation of democracy by appealing to cultural relativism and context sensitivity.

This is a familiar advocacy. It had earlier been prayed in aid in an effort to counter calls for the recognition, promotion, and protection of human rights in Africa.[84] The pith of that advocacy is that democracy and human rights have a variable content, their implementation being influenced by factors such as history, culture, the environment, and so on. This rationalization is of doubtful merit. Nevertheless, it betrays resistance by Africa's rulers to adopt those proven universal values.

The result is that damaging corruption, brazen election rigging, gross and widespread human rights abuses, and increased poverty continue to be the order of the day in Africa. So alarming are the scale of pauperization and the depth of social dislocation that there is widespread despondency and disaffection among the general population of every country. The idea of a nation-state is now clearly a big joke.

Most African states were pressurized into holding multi-party and periodic elections. Those elections should have been the onset of the

---

[84] C Anyangwe, 'Human Rights: Generations, Holism and Relativity,' (1993-1996) 25-28 *Zambia Law Journal* 81.

process of democratization and genuine, free and fair elections. This has not happened because African rulers have not fully and honestly subscribed to the idea of democracy. In almost every African country the political environment remains as disabling as ever. The political playing field is not yet level. Individuals still feel unsafe in their own countries. Civil society is still unable to flourish. Non-governmental organizations are still harassed and dissent is still not accommodated. There are still refugee flows and internal displacements in Africa, as if the entire continent is continually at war. Government still does not carry out its core business responsibly, effectively and transparently. African political leadership is yet to build a capable state. It is yet to build a state in which its component identities experience and share a sense of common belonging and identity, and have a feeling of equal and active citizenship.

Some African countries may have achieved independence. But *uhuru* is still to come. Others may have achieved independence. But they are yet to be decolonized. Others still may have achieved independence. But they have sunk into the abyss of pristine communal self-destruction. The state is a big joke, the nation a pipe dream. Many countries that pass for multi-party states are in reality neo-one-party states in which the ruling party is a hegemonic or dominant party with total grip on power and all state institutions. It is one thing to legalise political pluralism. It is quite another thing to create democratic institutions and see to it that they deliver.

Some states are more honest (give the devil his due). They do not pretend to have embraced political pluralism. They have peculiar contraptions that pass for democracy, e.g. 'no party democracy', 'guided democracy', 'African socialism', 'African democracy'. The Africanised democracy is at best a pseudo-democracy, a pretended democracy. State institutions still remain captive to an all-powerful ruler. There are no credible checks and balances. The legislature and the judiciary have no teeth. The management of public affairs is still opaque. Human rights receive minimum protection.

# Soldiers gun for political power

Watching the neo-patrimonial state from the side-lines are the state's own soldiers who, quite early in the day, developed a curious interest in this bandit system of government. It is the soldiers who guard the ruler, his family, his office, his house, and the national treasury. It is the soldiers who execute the ruler's sane and insane orders against the people. The soldiers were therefore the very first to notice the ruler's predilection for conspicuous consumption, his plunder of the national coffers, his excessive powers, the illegitimacy of his rule, his isolation from the people, and the gangrenous corruption of his regime.

The military observed in particular that the ruler, for all his outward appearance as a 'strongman' barking out commands and issuing decrees, is in fact lonely and vulnerable and dependent exclusively on the military who control and monopolize the state's instruments of terror. The African ruler in fact has feet of clay. This is his Achilles' heel. The military therefore lost no time in shooting their way through to State House amidst popular jubilation. The legitimizing rhetoric has always been the self-appointed mission of the military to prevent the state from ruin and perdition, to clean up the rot, and quickly restore constitutional rule.

The military in Africa have since stayed in the lucrative business of taking over government mafia-like, vaunting an ability to instil solutions by coup d'état. Whether a coup is politically or militarily inspired, ousting and capturing the African ruler has never called for exceptional military skills and lion-hearted soldiers. It is as simple as picking a louse from dirty hair. That in itself speaks volumes about the nature and foundation of the African state and its institutions as well as the ruler's powers. The enduring power of the military in African affairs represents the rejection, by those in arms, of the democratic principle of civilian supremacy in politics and the subordination of the military to the civil power.

The military have by word and conduct repeated *ad nauseum* that they desire to be part of the decision-making process in the state. In other words they feel there is no legitimate reason for keeping the military out of politics. In reaction to this sentiment there is now a growing tendency for military-civilian power-sharing in a number of African states. Some believe this might be one way of exorcising the continent of the demon of military coups. This is doubtful. Power-sharing may whet and has simply whetted the appetite of the military for more power. If they can get 100% power why would they settle for partial power? In any event the soldiers who are co-opted into government do not share their salaries and perks with the rest of the soldiers in the barracks. So co-opting a few military officers into the rulership of the country does not prevent and has never prevented a coup.

The first soldiers who took over government were initially hailed as messiahs, latter-day liberators. Even today some coups are considered as 'curative'; something like mandatory surgery for a patient at high risk of death. Coup leaders who carry out such coups are lionized. But more often than not the military rulers have turned out to be no less 'pirates in power' than the ousted civilian ruler. It follows that governance in Africa whether under civilians or the military is the same bad rule. Many have wondered what it is in the African State House that invariably turns its tenant from a human being into something not too far removed from an animal.

Where then should the eternally abused people of Africa turn for quality leadership? This is the millennium question. In a legitimate burst of anger, some African watchers have proposed a minimum 25-year re-colonisation or UN trusteeship of some identified African states on the sufficient ground that they were granted independence rather pre-maturely. To be sure that is a daring proposal. Others have proposed a re-configuration of the state in Africa along ethnic nationalities, on the model of the Swiss cantons, all under an overarching African Union continental government. This is equally a bold proposal. Both proposals do merit closer examination by Africa's thinking heads.

# Bibliography

## Articles and Book Chapters

Amissah ANE, 'The Role of the Judiciary in the Governmental Process: Ghana's Experience,' (1976) 13 *African Law Studies* 4.

Anyangwe C, 'Human Rights: Generations, Holism and Relativity,' (1993-1996) 25-28 *Zambia Law Journal* 81.

Anyangwe C, Good Governance, Democracy and Corruption in Africa, in: Simigiannis & Letlojane (ed.), *Human Rights Theories and Practices*, HURISA, Johannesburg, 2001, p. 215.

Anyangwe C, 'The Invasion of Iraq: Challenge to the Charter Prohibition of Violence in Inter-State Relations,' (2003) 28 (2) *Journal of Juridical Sciences* 58.

Anyangwe C, 'The Constitutive Act of the African Union,' (2006) 38 *Zambia Law Journal* 43.

Anyangwe C, Understanding the Phenomena of Unconstitutional Changes of Government in Africa, in: SBO Gutto (ed.), *Shared Values, Constitutionalism and Democracy in Africa*, Fortune-Publishing Africa, Johannesburg, 2011, p. 26.

Baregu M, 'Parliamentary Oversight of Defence and Security in Tanzania's Multiparty Parliament,' (2004) *Guarding the Guardians* 33, 39, available at http://www.iss.co.za/pubs/Books/guardiansaug04/Baregu.pdf

Birmingham D., 'The Twenty-Seventh of May: An Historical Note on the Abortive 1977 Coup in Angola,' (1978) 77 (309) *African Affairs* 554.

Blayton OH, 'African Coup d'état: the sequel – and the rule of law', 28 December 2008, available at http://www.africaloft.com

Bowett DW, 'Self-Determination and Political Rights in the Developing Countries,' *Proceedings of the American Society of International Law*, 1966, p. 133.

Date-Bah SK, 'Jurisprudence's Day in Court in Ghana', (1971) 20 *International and Comparative Law Quarterly* 317

Dias RWM, 'The UDI Case: The *Grundnorm* in Travail,' (1967) *Cambridge Law Journal* 5.

Engdahl, 'Soldiers, Riots and Revolutions: The Use of Military Troops in Civil Disorders,' (1971) 57 *Iowa L. Rev.* 1.

Eweluka DIO, 'The Military System of Administration in Nigeria,' (1974) 10 African Law Studies 75.

Feaver PD, "The Civil-Military Problematique: Huntington, Janowitz and the Question of Civilian Control," (1996) 23 (2) *Armed Forces and Society* 149.

Franck TM, 'The Emerging Right to Democratic Governance,' (1992) 86 *American Journal of International Law* 56.

Ghai Y, 'Coups and Constitutional Doctrines: The Role of Courts,' (1987) 58 (3) *Political Quarterly* 308.

Hahlo HR, 'The Privy Council and the "Gentle Revolution",' (1969) 86 *South African Law Journal* 419.

Hopton TC, 'Grundnorm and Constitution: The Legitimacy of Politics,' (1978) 24 *McGill Law Journal* 72.

Hutchful E, 'Demilitarising the Political Process in Africa: Some Basic Issues,' *African Security Review* 1997.

Luanda N, The Tanganyika Rifles and the Mutiny of January 1961, in: Hutchful & Bathily (ed.), *The Military and Militarism in Africa*, CODESRIA, Dakar, 1998, p. 175.

Lupogo H, 'Civil-Military Relations and Political Stability in Tanzania,' (2001) 10 (1) *African Security Review* 33.

Macfarlane LJ, 'Pronouncing on Rebellion: the Rhodesian Courts and U.D.I.,' (1969) 12 *Public Law* 324.

McGowan PJ, 'Coups and Conflicts in West Africa, 1955-2004: Part I, Theoretical Perspectives', (2005) 32 *Society & Armed Forces* 5, 'Part II, Empirical Findings', (2006) 32 *Society & Armed Forces* 234.

McGowan PJ, 'African military coups d'état, 1956-2001: frequency, trends and distribution,' (2003) 41 (3) *Journal of Modern African Studies* 351.

Meeks CI, 'Illegal law enforcement: aiding civil authorities in violation of the Posse Comitatus Act,' (1975) 70 *Military Law Review* 83.

Mindua A, 'L'ONU face aux coups d'état militaries et aux gouvernements non-démocratiques,' (1994) 6 *RADIC* 209.

N'Diaye B, 'How not to Institutionalize Civilian Control: Kenya's Coup Prevention Strategies, 1964-1997,' (2002) 28 *Society & Armed Forces* 619.

Ngoma N, Civil-Military Relations: Searching for a Conceptual Framework with an African Bias, in: G. Chileshe et al (ed.), *Civil-Military Relations in Zambia*, Institute for Security Studies, Pretoria, 2004, p. 3.

Ochoche SA, The Military and National Security in Africa, in: E Hutchful & A Bathily (ed.), *The Military and Militarism in Africa*, CODESRIA, 1998, p. 105.

Ojo A, 'The Search for a Grundnorm in Nigeria – The *Lakanmi* Case,' (1971) 20 I.C.L.Q. 117

Omoigui, N, 'Preventing Coups in Nigeria,' available at http://www.gamji.com/nowa/nowa21.htm

Palley C, 'The Judicial Process: UDI and the Southern Rhodesian Judiciary,' (1967) 30 *Mod. L. R.* 263.
Sawer G, 'Political Questions,' (1963) 15 *U. of Toronto L.J.* 49.

Souare I, *The AU and the Challenge of Unconstitutional Changes of Government in Africa,* Institute for Security Studies, 2009.

The New York Times, 11 August 1982, '145 were Killed in Kenyan Uprising.'

The New York Times, 22 August 1982, 'Kenya Disbands the Air Force after Coup Bid.'

The New York Times, 11 February 1988, 'South Africa Quells Coup Attempt in a Homeland.'

The New York Times, 8 March 1990, 'Turmoil Spreads to 2nd Homeland.'

Welsh RS, 'The Constitutional Case in Southern Rhodesia,' (1967) 83 *L. Q. R.* 64.

Weston MF, 'Political Questions,' (1925) 38 *H.L.R.* 296

Wharam A, 'Treason in Rhodesia,' (1967) *Camb. L. J.* 189.

# Books

Afrifa AA, *The Ghana Coup, 24 February 1966,* Frank Cass, London, 1966 pp. 85-86, 124.

Chileshe et al. (ed.), *Civil-Military Relations in Zambia*, Institute for Social Security, Pretoria, 2004.

Connor K & Hebditch, D, *How to Stage a Military Coup from Planning to Execution*, Pen & Sword Books, 2008

Cox TS, *Civil-Military Relations in Sierra Leone: A Case Study of African Soldiers in Politics*, Harvard University Press, Cambridge Mass., 1976.

Deltombe T et al., *Kamerun! Une Guerre Cachée aux Origines de la Françafrique 1948-1971*, La Découverte, Paris, 2011.

Desch CM, *Civilian Control of the Military: The Changing Security Environment,* Johns Hopkins University Press, 2001.

Feaver PD, *Armed Servants: Agency, Oversight, and Civil-Military Relations*, Harvard University Press, 2005.

Finer SE, *The Man on Horseback: The Role of the Military in Politics*, Transaction Publishers, 2002.

Freeman MDA, *Lloyd's Introduction to Jurisprudence*, Sweet & Maxwell, London, 2001

Ferguson C, *Coup d'état: A Practical Manual*, Arms & Armour Press, Dorset, 1987.

Gaillard P, *Ahidjo – Patriote et Despôte, Bâtisseur de l'Etat Camerounais*, Jeune Afrique Livre, Paris, 1994.

Goodspeed JD, *Six Coups d'Etat*, Viking Press, New York, 1962;

Huntington SP, *The Soldier and the State: The Theory and Politics of Civil-Military Relations*, Belknap Press, 1981.

Janowitz M, *The Professional Soldier*, Free Press, 1964.

Luttwak E, *Coup d'état: A Practical Handbook*, Harvard University Press, 1980.

Malaparte C, *Techniques du Coup d'Etat*, Paris, 1931.

Mazrui A, & Tidy M, *Nationalism and New States in Africa*, East African Educational Publishers, Nairobi, 1984, p. 261.

McCarthy S, *Africa: The Challenge of Transformation*, London, 1994, p. 106

Rubin N & Cotran E (ed.), *Annual Survey of African Law*, vol. 4, Frank Cass, London, 1970, p. 28.

Sampford C and Palmer M, *The Theory of Collective Response*, Lexington Books, 2005.

Shivji IG, *Pan-Africanism or Pragmatism? Lessons of Tanganyika-Zanzibar Union*, *Mkuki na Nyoka* Publishers, Dar es Salam, 2008.

Smith W, *We Must Run While They Walk: A Portrait of Africa's Julius Nyerere*, New York, Random House, 1971.

# Cases

Aksionairenoye Obschestvo, Luther v. James Sagor & Company [1921] 3 K.B. 532

Asma Jilani v. The Government of Punjab & Anor, PLD 1972 SC 139

Att-Gen. v. Mustafa Ibrahim (1964) Cyprus L. R. 195

Bengum Nusrat Bhutto v. Federation of Pakistan, PLD 1977 SC 657

Bhutto v. The State, PLD 1978 SC 40.

Lakanmi & Kikelomo v. A-G, W. Nigeria (1971) 5 Nigerian Lawyers Quarterly 133

Lardner-Burke v. Madzimbamuto [1968] 2 S.A.L.R. 284 (Rhodesia)

Luther v. Borden, 7 Howard 1 (1848)

Makotso & Ors v. King Moshoeshoe II & Ors (1988) Lesotho unreported case.

Mitchell v. DPP [1985] LRC (Const.) 127 (Grenada)

Sallah v. The Attorney General for Ghana (1970) Current Cases Special Reference No. 1 of 1955, PLD 1955 F.C. 435

The State v. Dosso (1958), PLD 1958 SC 533.

Uganda v. Commissioner of Prisons, Exparte Matovu (1966) E.A. 514

Valabhazi v. Controller of Taxes (1981) Seychelles Civil Appeal, unreported.

## Documents

African Charter on Human and peoples' Rights, 1981
International Covenant on Civil and Political Rights, 1966
International Covenant on Economic, Social and Cultural Rights,
    1966
Posse Comitatus Act, 1970, 18 U.S.C. $1385 (1970)
UNGA Res A/RES/32/105N of 14 December 1977
Universal Declaration of Human Rights, 1948


## Websites

http://allafrica.com/africa
http://en.wikipedia.org/wiki/civilian
http://en.wikipedia.org/wiki/Civilian_control_of_the_military.
http://www.africaloft.com
http://www.essortment.com/
http://www.gamji.com/nowa/nowa21.htm
http://www.iss.co.za/dynamic/administration/
http://www.iss.co.za/pubs/ASR/6No2/Hutchful.html
http://www.iss.co.za/pubs/Books/guardiansaug04/Baregu.pdf
http://www.nation.co.ke/News
http://www.soros.org/initiatives/washington/